Contents

Sight & Sound

TEACHERS' MANUAL

VISUAL AID TO MELODY AND HARMONY

A

ARPAD DARAZS

STEPHEN JAY

BOOSEY & HAWKES, INC.

Oceanside, New York

46684

Printed in U.S.A.

PREFACE

"Sight and Sound" is devoted to the development of musicianship through the ear and the voice. By awakening the ear and using it as the central tool for teaching and experiencing music we can prepare the way for instrumental training as well as for intelligent and more enjoyable music listening.

Such aural training must be more widely undertaken at the younger age levels, for it is only too clear that our music classes in colleges and conservatories are filled with young adults who have been ill equipped to pursue their musical studies. Therefore, it is to the "pre-teens" that the authors have directed their efforts in *this* book.

"Sight and Sound" has been developed with the aid and encouragement of many people. The authors wish to thank the following persons to whom a special expression of gratitude is due:

To Zoltan Kodaly, who provided the initial inspiration for this course and whose similar ear training system is in use throughout Hungary.

To Harris Danziger, Director of the Third Street Music School Settlement in New York City in whose "Musicianship Classes" much of the specific material for this book has been developed, and who has provided the opportunity for the authors to train others to use this system.

To Father Raphael, O.S.B. pastor of St. Killian's Roman Catholic Church in Farmingdale, Long Island. With his active cooperation, this ear training system has been used to train the famous St. Killian's Boy Choir which he founded. Through his efforts, this choir has widely demonstrated the method.

To Hugh Ross, Director of the Schola Cantorum, who did so much to bring our system to the attention of other musicians, and to our many colleagues, too many to be named individually, who have tested this material in their classrooms and studios and with their choirs — we express our deepest gratitude.

The authors further wish gratefully to acknowledge the efforts of Professors Martin Bernstein and Harold J. Heeremans of New York University and professor Harry Wilson of Teacher's College, Columbia University. As chairmen of the respective Music Departments they have encouraged the authors in their use of this material at the college level.

INTRODUCTION

SIGHT AND SOUND is a progressive method of aural training. Since music is an aural art, there can be no better way to approach the study and enjoyment of it than by using the ear as the vehicle for study. This course utilizes the following techniques to pursue its goals:

a) Properly selected and graded materials in the presentation and drill of each teaching point.

b) A special presentation of the "moveable" syllables designed to instill a feeling for the movement and relationships of musical sounds.

c) A series of hand signals which represent the musical sounds and involves the student physically in the interpretation of music.

d) A systematic presentation of the rhythmic elements of music.

Ear Training and Musicianship

Developing the ear to perceive and remember relationships of musical sounds and patterns constitutes the method called Ear Training, the primary tool by which all the elements of musicianship are to be taught. There are three phases to the ear training process: the *hearing* of the sound, the *acceptance* of that sound, and the *reproduction* of the sound. Ear training must be taught primarily through melody which is the essence of music. Everything else, even harmonic constructions, are outgrowths of melody and are of secondary importance in developing the ear.

It is through Ear Training that the theory of music, intervals, scales, chords, etc., can be taught in a far more interesting and meaningful way. Such an approach to the general study of music also simplifies the job of the instrumental teacher who usually has too little time even for the technical instruction necessary in instrumental teaching. Finally, Ear Training not only produces lasting benefits to future generations of intelligent music listeners, but also lays the foundation necessary for further study by our future musicians. The time to guide and develop the ear is at an early age and not at the college level, as is too often the case.

The three elements of this aural training in SIGHT AND SOUND can be defined as:

a) *Sight Singing* — the ability to translate symbols (music notation) into the musical sounds they represent.

b) *Dictation* — the ability to translate musical sounds into their written symbols.

c) *Rhythm* — the ability to recognize and notate the rhythms which "transport" the musical sounds of a composition.

This new course of SIGHT AND SOUND is similar to the ear training system currently used nationally in Hungary under the direction of Zoltan Kodaly. Its roots lie in the work of an Englishman, John Curwen (1816-80), whose "Tonic Sol-Fa" principles have been redeveloped by Kodaly. Utilizing techniques of both Curwen and Kodaly, the authors have developed the present course to meet the specific needs and musical traditions of the English-speaking community. It employs the use of syllables (solmization), hand signals which are used to express the musical sounds, and a dynamic presentation of rhythm.

SOLMIZATION

Many attempts have been made to label the various musical sounds to make them easier to remember and relate to other notes. The use of arbitrary syllable names to represent musical sounds originated in the eleventh century with Guido d'Arezzo. He used the syllables, which began the successive phrases of a Latin Hymn to St. John — *Ut, Re, Mi, Fa, Sol* and *La,* to represent the six tones of the hexachord. *("Mi-Fa"* indicated a position of the semi-tone within *any* hexachord.) Before this time, melodies were "passed" from teacher to pupil or generation to generation by rote. The use of Guido's syllables made a practical method for sight singing.

The substitution of *Do* in place of the less resonant sounding *Ut* was accomplished by 1672 in Italy. The use of the syllable *Si* for the added seventh note of a scale can be traced to 1611. In some countries the syllable *Ti* has replaced the *Si* to avoid having two syllables begin with the same initial letter (*Sol* and *Si*) and, also, because of the use of *Si* as a chromatic syllable (see page 10). In addition, the final "l" of *Sol* is sometimes omitted for simplicity of diction (to avoid the double consonants in *Sol-la*) and to keep all syllables to two letters. With these few changes and additions, Guido's naming system has survived until our present day.

The traditional syllable names of the musical notes *(Do, Re, Mi, Fa, So, La* and *Ti)* are now used in two different ways. In the "Fixed Do" system, which is used particularly in France and Italy, C is always called *Do,* D is *Re,* E is *Mi,* etc. In many other countries the "Moveable Do" system is employed. In this system, the first note of *any* major scale is called *Do* the second *Re* the third *Mi,* etc.

One other system in use today must be mentioned,—the application of numbers "One, Two, Three, Four, Five, Six and Seven" to indicate the degrees of the scale. This system also goes back a long way, its origin having been traced to as early as 1665. It has been used by many people including a disciple of the noted Swiss educator Pestalozzi, Hans Georg Nageli (1773-1836) who printed melodies in "figure notation." In the "Galin-Paris-Chevé" System Pierre Galin (1786-1821), Aime Paris (1798-1866), Emile Chevé (1804-1864), the numbers were to be looked at while singing with moveable syllables. It might also be pointed out that Dr. Lowell Mason (1792-1872) printed songs in both syllable and number notation.

COMPARISON OF TONAL LABELING SYSTEMS

Let us use the familiar song, "Three Blind Mice" with each of these labeling systems.

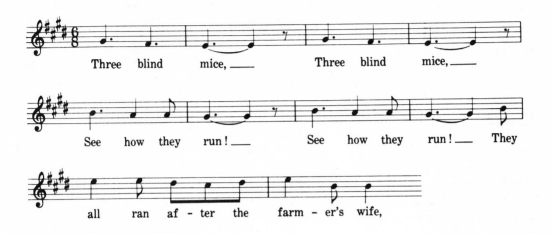

1. The "Fixed Do" System

Sing the song in the following manner:

The syllables used in this manner do not take into account that all of the F's, C's, G's, and D's in the key of E Major are "sharped." Nor is there any differentiation between G, G sharp, or G Flat, a fact which the student is expected to keep in mind. This is too advanced a concept and the syllables actually have nothing to do with hearing.

The system may be used, however, with chromatic syllable names. Thus **So** (G), when raised by a sharp sign, becomes **Si**; F sharp becomes **Fi** instead of **Fa**. Sing the song with chromatic syllables:

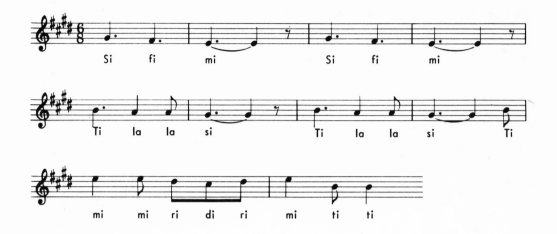

But this again is putting a meaningless label on the sounds. In the United States and England, as well as many other countries, "fixed" syllables are not the musical alphabet of the musical language. In these countries, the actual names of the notes may be used:

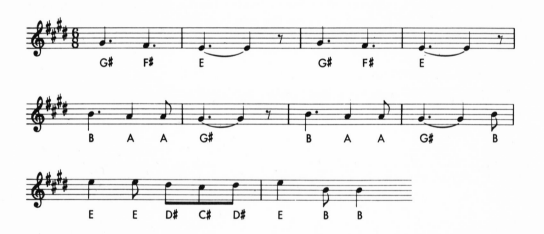

Therefore, the "Fixed Do" system offers no advantages at this stage. It forces the student to learn an additional set of extraneous letter names and does nothing to clarify the sounds. It is of no use in the crucial task of ear training, that is, expressing the interval relationships between the notes within the tonality. The use of the "Fixed Do" system would mean, as is so often done, that the key of C Major must be used for quite some time during the early stages of ear and musicianship training. The authors feel that this practice is fraught with danger to the ear and subscribe to John Curwen's view that "as the keytone in music does move, it is much wiser to let our signs and symbols move with it."

2. Number System

Sing the song with the notes of its scale numbered as follows:

10

Three two one, three two one,

five four four three, five four four three, five

eight eight seven six seven eight five five,

It will be seen that the numbers provide the same system of relationships between the notes of the scale as do the "moveable syllables," but they are difficult to sing. The numbers in the English language contain constricting throat sounds such as "thr*ee*," "*fi*ve," "*ei*ght," etc., and in the case of the important seventh note of the scale (leading tone) the number has two syllables — "sev-en." These various factors combine to make it impossible to sing at even moderate speed. It must also be pointed out that the numbers do not accurately depict the intervals. For example, 5-3 in a major key is minor third, yet 5-3 in a minor scale is a major third.

3. "Moveable Do" System

Finally, sing the song with the "moveable" syllable names:

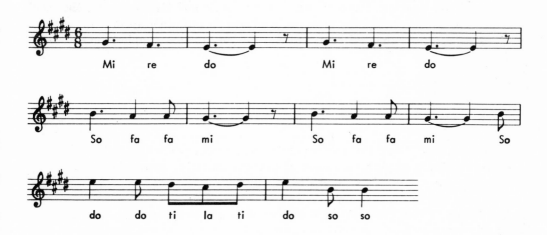

Mi re do Mi re do

So fa fa mi So fa fa mi So

do do ti la ti do so so

The syllable names are far easier to produce vocally and are easier to remember musically than are numbers. We are also able to utilize any key within vocal range instead of having to use only that of C major. The same syllables would be used in any key because the distances between the notes of the scale remain the same. In other words, interval and chordal patterns are clarified through the use of the "Moveable Do" system.

John Curwen's "Tonic Sol-Fa System" provides the basis of today's "Moveable Do" system. He adapted it from a "sol-fa" system developed by Miss Sarah Ann Glover (1785-1867). By means of a "modulator" (a chart upon which the syllables were placed in proper order) the teacher would point to the syllables, the students responding by singing. Curwen believed this was desirable in place of the regular notation. The authors feel that the use of syllable names is a valuable interpretation of, rather than a substitution for, the regular music notation.

The "Moveable Do" method provides the best, quickest and safest basis for the training of the ear. The relationship of each tone to the keytone and to the other tonal members of the key are best clarified through the use of this system. We might remind the reader that Guido's original syllables were "moveable." The "Moveable Do" method is especially practical for the average student since it interprets the character and mental effect of the tones within the key better than any other system. After all, music is composed not of individual notes but of a series of notes related to a central key. Only after these relationships are thoroughly assimilated through the "Moveable Do" system, should any "Fixed Do" concepts be introduced.

ORDER OF SYLLABLE PRESENTATION

As established by Kodaly, the syllables are presented in a special order which has been designed to develop the ear gradually. Each sound is presented through a piece of music which uses the tonal material under examination. This is done either through a very familiar song, or through one which is first taught by imitation (rote).

Through its popular usage we know that the **So** and **Mi** are among the most frequently used of sounds. This interval is employed prominently in a great variety of songs and instrumental compositions ranging from a simple "Cuckoo Call",

Cuc - koo

to Mozart.

The **So-Mi** interval is particularly easy to remember and reproduce and, therefore, they are the first sounds presented. This method is a departure from the usual practice of first presenting the **Do** but it is far simpler to assimilate.

The next sound presented is the **La,** which produces a pattern familiar to children the world over:

Only then is the **Do** presented. With the addition of the **Re** we have reached the first, crucial goal of ear training, the Pentatonic Scale(refer to Unit Seven).

PENTATONIC SCALE

The **La-So-Mi-Re-Do** syllables form the Pentatonic (five tone) scale, the basis for extraordinary amounts of strangely appealing folk music from diverse cultures. Of special interest to Americans is the manner in which this scale is used in Southern Spirituals, Western Cowboy Songs, and in the great wealth of folk music inherited from the British Isles.

The Pentatonic Scale employs no half steps and it is extremely important that the syllables which create these (**Fa** and **Ti**) are not presented until the pentatonic material is well absorbed. The tones of the Pentatonic Scale are the pillars upon which the major and minor scales are built. When the student is thoroughly familiar with the sounds of the Pentatonic Scale, the simple addition of the **Fa** and **Ti** will produce both the major and (natural) minor scale forms.

RHYTHM

It is important that rhythm be presented as naturally as possible, for it is the feeling of motion and the flow of the beat which must be instilled in the student. The note values which are presented first in this course are those which give a feeling of natural movement — the quarter and eighth notes rather than the whole and half notes. The latter are easy to present theoretically, but they are too static in sound.

A method of saying the rhythm is used with the word "Tah" representing the longer note value (quarter) and the word "Tee" representing the shorter note value (eighth). It will be seen that the vowel sound "ah" is in a lower vocal range than that of "ee." While the jaw must take the time to drop in order to produce the word "tah," a mere flick of the tongue is all that is necessary to say "tee." These verbalizations of the note values are fitted into a framework of tapping, clapping and finally, conducting.

Rhythm, just as pitch, is therefore expressed by "syllables." It can be dictated independently from pitch and can be used for creative composition and ensemble training.

Hand Signals

The hand signals used in SIGHT AND SOUND are the direct descendants of hand "postures" developed by John Curwen in 1870. The idea of using the hand to describe sound has been used throughout the centuries. Even Guido used a stationary hand to represent his hexachord. The authors present a revised set of Curwen hand signals as the best way to involve the student physically in the interpretation and reproduction of musical sounds.

Hand Signal Chart

ORIGINAL CURWEN SIGNALS   **SIGHT AND SOUND — REVISED SIGNALS**

DO    DO

TI    TI  TA

LA    LA

Thumb held down for **So**, raised for **Si**   SI

SO    SO  FI

Revised Signal for **Fa** is used, Thumb down is for **Fa**, the opposite (thumb up) is for **Fi**

FA    FA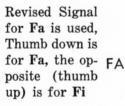

MI      MI

RE    RE

DO    DO

14

The authors have created signals for the very common chromatic tone, **Si**, **Fi** and **Ta.**

Each signal represents a tone of the scale. It not only illustrates the general height or depth of the sound by moving the hand up or down, but also, by the shape of the hand signal, "acts out" the function of that tone within the scale structure. The tones of a scale are of either *stable* or *active* quality. The **So, Mi** and **Do** are *stable* whereas the **La, Re, Fa** and **Ti** are *active*. The hand signals describe these qualities and, by involving body movement on the part of the listener or singer, enables the student to participate in the sound in an active way. In singing, the hand signals are used to support the sound and intonation. In dictation, the sound is first expressed through the body by the hand signals and then translated into symbols. The signals also make possible the early introduction of part singing. This is important because it is only through part singing, not unison, that intonation can be taught.

The use of hand signals has made it possible for many students of limited musical hearing to sing and take musical dictation. In the experience of the authors there is no such thing as a totally tone deaf child.

How to Use the Manuals

We believe that the student should see only that which is educationally necessary. For that reason the Students' Manual does not have music to the rote songs; time signatures are simplified ($2 = \dfrac{2}{4}; \; 3 = \dfrac{3}{4}$, etc.) ; instead of key signatures the students see only the position of **Do** or **So** on the staff. Thus the student will see only that which can be comprehended at each level.

THE UNIT

Each unit contains a song from which are extracted tonal or rhythmic materials for presentation. Every unit has pitch and rhythm drills, singing exercises and dictation material. All are designed to reinforce the same teaching points. The Teachers' Manual contains "Suggested Procedures" for teaching which are merely guides for the creative teacher. We expect you to improvise freely upon these.

There is no precise way of indicating the exact amount of time needed to cover the material of a unit. This will depend upon the period of time devoted to the lesson per week which differs from school to school. If this method is to be used as a part of a larger course (General Music, for example), the material in each unit must be subdivided. A unit is not meant to be covered in a single session but as a general rule should not take longer than three meetings. Some units will naturally be assimilated more quickly than others.

A suggested assignment has been provided for each unit. While this is meant only as a guide to the teacher, it does indicate the importance of a properly balanced assignment in the learning structure. Every assignment emphasizes the rhythm and tonal points of the lesson, and requires of the student some type of creative expression. Such assignments are a positive asset to the learning experience.

MELODIC PRESENTATION

Presentation of songs should be vocal; only the voice can convey both words and music instantaneously. While it is true that instruments can be useful in accompaniment and dictation, they should not be used for presentation of melody. In particular, the piano should be avoided. Use of a piano which is not in tune can actually be damaging to the ear. Sparingly used, any instrument which the teacher knows well, such as the recorder or violin, can enrich the material presented.

STARTING PITCHES

It is important to vocal health to start upon a proper pitch — a tone that will place the entire melody within proper vocal range. This is dependent upon age, experience and even time of day. For example, if the ear training is done early in the morning the voice should be started in a lower range than would be necessary later in the day.

Starting tones should be varied. After using one tonal center for a while, the teacher should change to another. A single melody drill can be done from several starting places. This both benefits the vocal chords physically and sharpens the ear.

The following ranges of starting pitches are generally suitable for children from about 8-13 years of age. The teacher's experience will tell which are the best ranges at any given time.

So-Mi	(Unit One)	**So** = f, f sharp, g
So-Mi-Do	(Unit Three)	**So** = f sharp, g, g sharp, a
La-So-Mi-Re-Do	(Units Four-Five)	**So** = f sharp, g, g sharp, a
Low **La**	(Unit Six)	**Do** = d, e flat, e, f
High **Do**	(Unit Eight)	High **Do** should not exceed high d or e

HAND SIGNALS

The signals should be presented with the teacher's *left* hand, while the students imitate them with their *right* hands. This allows the student to make a mirror-like imitation which is easier for them to duplicate. The **So** hand signal should be made at chest level. All other signals must show their approximate distance up or down, **Mi** by lowering the hand, **La** by raising it, etc.

The teacher can try two-part hand signals (see Unit Five) in order to introduce elementary two-part singing. It also makes possible the improvisation of intervals, and is a wonderful tool for teaching correct intonation.

The hand signals also provide a fine method for instantaneously creating melodies without the intervention of written symbols on the board. Needless to say they also provide an additional tool for class discipline because the children are always participating when hand signals are being used.

16

RHYTHM PRESENTATION

As will be seen throughout the manual, two-part rhythm drills can be done in many interesting ways. The following ideas suggest possible approaches to two-part work:

a) The class is divided into two groups.

b) Two individuals can be chosen, or they can volunteer.

c) The drill can be done by one person (the class in unison) with the right hand doing the upper part and the left hand doing the lower part. This requires a great deal of coordination and should be attempted only after considerable practice.

d) The drills may be performed by tapping one part with a hand and stepping the other part.

TEACHING THE SYLLABLES

Each new syllable is presented in the manuals as follows:

a) The sound is presented through a song which is either familiar or learned by imitation. The specific melodic element is then derived from the song; the relationships between the new and previously learned syllable patterns are examined. Finally the new element is given its musical name.

b) The sound of the syllable is then shown on the staff as a visual reminder and the hand signal is taught to provide a physical reminder of the sound.

c) The new element is then drilled with hand signals, syllable exercises, notation and dictation.

TEACHING SONGS

In teaching songs by any of the following three methods (Rote, Syllables, Notes), we leave to the teacher the specific motivating devices which are so necessary in the introduction of songs.

Teaching By Rote

Rote is defined as the imitation of the teacher's performance by the student. Songs learned in this manner have actually been dictated by the teacher though the sounds have not been written down by the student. The natural talent of children to imitate is used to develop melodic and rhythmic memory.

1. The teacher first sings the entire song.

2. The teacher then sings the first section (not exceeding two to four measures). The students then imitate (sing back) the section which is repeated until it has been memorized.

3. The teacher then sings the next section and the students imitate until memorized.

4. The teacher sings the combined first and second sections which are then sung back by the students.

5. The teacher then continues with the third and following sections. The students imitate as in the above directions.

Model rote song

Using "Coral" from Unit Four as an example, let us follow our step-by-step method of teaching a rote song.

Sing the entire song.

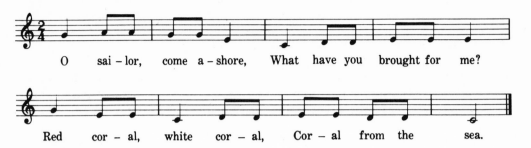

O sai – lor, come a – shore, What have you brought for me?

Red cor – al, white cor – al, Cor – al from the sea.

Sing the first section; students repeat it.

O sai – lor, come a – shore,

Repeat until memorized.

Sing the second section; students repeat until memorized.

What have you brought for me?

Sing sections one and two; students imitate.

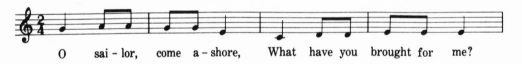

O sai – lor, come a – shore, What have you brought for me?

Sing the third section; students repeat until memorized.

Red cor – al, white cor – al,

Sing the fourth section; students repeat until memorized.

Cor – al from the sea.

Sing sections three and four; students imitate.

Red   cor – al,   white   cor – al,   Cor – al   from the   sea.

Sing the entire song; students repeat the entire song.

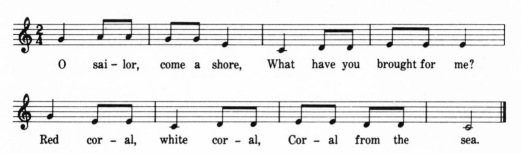

O   sai – lor,   come a   shore,   What   have you   brought for   me?

Red   cor – al,   white   cor – al,   Cor – al   from the   sea.

Teaching by Syllables

In this style of presentation, the syllables and rhythm are placed above the text. This fills in the wide gap between rote learning and singing from the notes on the staff. It provides a unique and vital intermediary step. Such material is included in the Singing Exercises in each unit which have songs and melodies with and without text.

For example, "Polly Wolly Doodle" would be written:

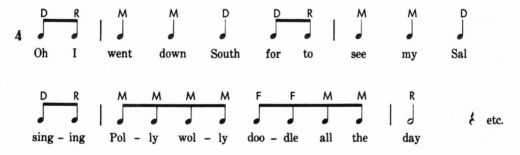

1. Read the text and explain the meaning, especially of unusual words.
2. Observe the time signature. Tap and say the rhythm. Then say the words in rhythm.
3. Sing the melody slowly with syllables without rhythm. Use hand signals.
4. Sing the melody with syllables in rhythm. The use of hand signals is optional.
5. Sing the melody in rhythm substituting a neutral sound ("lu," "lah" or hum) for the syllables.
6. Sing the melody substituting the words for the syllables.
7. Sing the melody with words while tapping the rhythm.
8. Sing the melody with words while conducting.

19

Teaching by Notes

1. Teacher first sings the entire song.
2. Show the location of **Do** on the staff.
3. Read the names of the notes (syllable names) without singing their pitch.
4. Melodic preparation. Practice the anticipated difficult intervals in the song. This can be done by writing all of the participating notes of the song in scale form on the board. The teacher then points to various notes while the class sings, thus forming drills which lead progressively to the difficult interval. For example, if the interval **La-Re** is in the song, the teacher can prepare a drill beginning with the simple **So-Mi** as in the following:

So-Mi; So-So-Mi-Re-Re; So-La-Re-Re; La-La-Re-La-Re

5. Sing the melody in syllables slowly without rhythm, section by section. Use hand signals.
6. From this point on, the instructions are the same as those for teaching by syllable.

Unit One

Surely the best way to approach music is through music. Introduce the lesson by suggesting the class sing this well known song.

AMERICA THE BEAUTIFUL

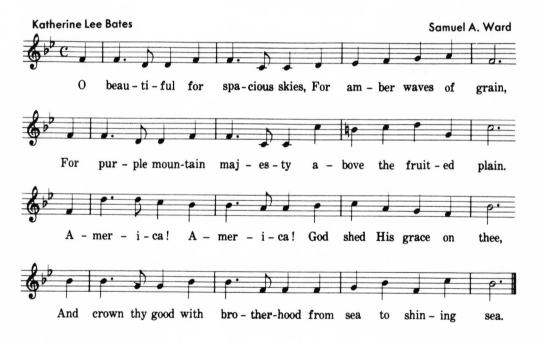

This particular song has been chosen because its opening tones alternate between **So** (the fifth note of the major scale) and **Mi** (the third note of the major scale):

SUGGESTIONS: PITCH

1. After the song has been sung, the class should hum the first four notes to determine that there is a repeated higher and lower sound.

2. Point out that these are easily remembered because so many other songs begin with the same two sounds. The following can be used as examples of songs which start with these sounds. They can also replace "America the Beautiful" as introductory songs for Unit One.

THE ARMY GOES ROLLING ALONG

CAMPTOWN RACES

Stephen Foster

The Camp-town la - dies   sing this song: Doo - dah!   Doo - dah!   The
I   come down there with my hat caved in,   Doo - dah!   Doo - dah!   I

Camp-town race track   five miles long,   Oh,   doo - dah   day!
go   back home with a pock-et full of tin, Oh,   doo - dah   day!

Goin' to run   all   night! Goin' to run all day!   I'll

bet my mon-ey on the bob - tail nag,   some-bod - y bet on the   bay.

2. The long-tail filly and the big black hoss,
   Doodah! Doodah!
   They fly the track and they both cut across,
   Oh, doodah day!
   The blind hoss stickin' in a big bog hole,
   Doodah! Doodah!
   Can't touch bottom with a ten foot pole,
   Oh, doodah day!

3. Old muley cow came onto the track,
   Doodah! Doodah!
   The bob-tail flung her over his back,
   Oh, doodah day!
   Then flew along like a railroad car,
   Doodah! Doodah!
   Runnin' a race with a shootin' star,
   Oh, doodah day!

ROTE SONG

Teach the new song, "What's Your Name?" (refer to Students' Manual, page 8). This is the first song in the Students' Manual.

"WHAT'S YOUR NAME?"

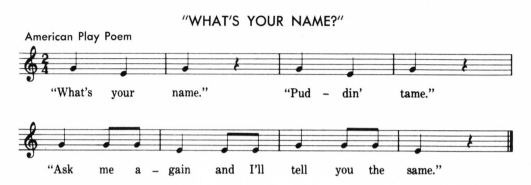

American Play Poem

"What's your name." "Pud – din' tame."

"Ask me a – gain and I'll tell you the same."

1. The teacher should encourage the students to listen for the rise and fall of the melody. The first three words are enough to convey the idea:

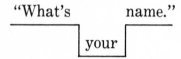

"What's   name."
                   your

2. The two sounds which are used in this song can be easily remembered because so many other songs also begin with the same two tones. For example, the class can sing the starting tones of "America The Beautiful" and be reminded that the entire song, "What's Your Name?" is made up of these two sounds.

3. Identify the upper tone as a sound called **So** and the lower tone as a sound called **Mi.** As the class sings "What's Your Name?" again, substitute the appropriate **So** or **Mi** for the words:

S M S   S M S   S S S M M M S S S M

4. Present the hand signals as a way we can "show" the melody with our hands. The teacher should hold the hand at chest level for the **So** and move the hand several inches lower for the **Mi.**

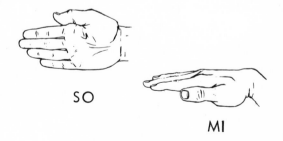

SO

MI

24

5. The students now sing "What's Your Name?" as they also make the hand signals. Their book illustrates how this should be done.
6. Encourage the class to supply the names of additional songs which begin with **So-Mi,** such as:

"Come Thou Almighty King" — first two tones

"Where Is My Little Dog Gone" — first three tones

"The Army Goes Rolling Along" — first nine tones

SINGING EXERCISES

The following Singing Exercises will be found in the Students' Manual page 9. The students must use hand signals while singing these drills:

a) S M S M S S S

b) S S M S M M

c) M S S M S S M S

Rhythm Presentation

The students' book introduces rhythm by calling it "The Musical Heartbeat." Perhaps the class could read aloud the two short paragraphs before you present the next song.

ROTE SONG

Teach another new song which uses only the tones **So** and **Mi.** The teacher may use his (her) own name instead of "Peter Pan."

SAY YOUR NAME

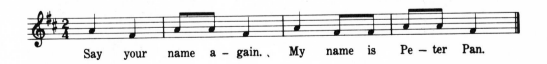

Say your name a – gain. ، My name is Pe – ter Pan.

1. The teacher can point to various members of the class who then sing the song substituting their own names for "Peter Pan."
2. While singing the song, a student may point to another boy or girl on the word "your". When he completes the song, having thereby introduced himself, the student who has been pointed to then sings the entire song and points to the next student, etc.

SUGGESTIONS: RHYTHM

1. The note values which are employed in Unit One are the quarter and eighth notes, rather than the slower ones. It is important to convey to the students the feeling of motion in musical rhythm. The quarter note connotes a "walking" feeling and the eighth notes a "running" one. There are many ways in which the longer and shorter rhythm sounds can be shown.

    a) The pendulum of a small clock swings twice while that of the large clock swings once:

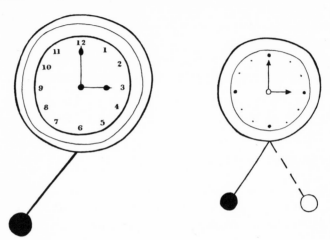

    b) When a small child walks he must take two steps to equal each one that his teacher takes:

    c) Instruct the class to:
        (1) Step 4 walking beats.
        (2) Step 8 running beats (twice as fast — 2 to each walking step.
        (3) Divide class into two sections, one section "walks" while other group "runs."

2. Have the students sing the rote song and instruct them to step *each* note as they sing.

    a) The class should now "walk" only four steps while singing two measures. In this way they will be "walking" only the quarter note beats. One student can indicate where the steps are taking place by writing a stroke on the blackboard while the class sings the song using just the sound "lah" for each note:

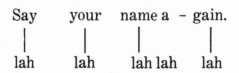

26

b) Have the class determine:

> How many "lah's" were sung on the first step. (Answer: one)
> How many "lah's" were sung on the second step. (Answer: one)
> How many "lah's" were sung on the third step. (Answer: two)

> Thus, the third step can be subdivided into two smaller ones.

3. The rhythm of a piece can be "said" by using the sound "tah" for the longer notes and "tee" for the shorter ones. The rhythm of the rote song can be "said" as follows:

Say	your	name a	- gain.	My	name is	Pe-ter	Pan.
tah	tah	tee tee	tah	tah	tee tee	tee tee	tah

(This diagram may help clarify that one "tah" equals two "tee" notes).

4. When writing the note values the students will use a straight line $|$ for the "tah" notes and an arc $\cap$ for the two "tee" notes. It can be pointed out that the actual notes would look like these:

tah notes: ♩ ♩   **tee** notes: ♫ ♫

For convenience we are merely using the upper part of the notes (the stems) and curving the connected eighth (tee) notes. For speed the students should be taught to write these note values with one movement of the pencil:

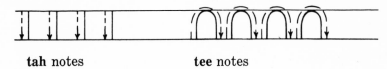

tah notes   **tee** notes

PROCEDURES FOR RHYTHMIC DICTATION

1. Clap the following rhythm pattern:

2. The students (either individual volunteers or the entire class) then clap the pattern from memory.
3. Ask someone to "say" the rhythm: "Tah tah tee-tee tah."
4. The entire class then "says" the rhythm.

5. The class now writes the rhythm pattern in their workbook (Students' Manual page 9):

6. Following the above procedures, use other rhythm patterns which utilize the "tah" and "tee" notes. The patterns should not exceed four quarter notes in length. Some possibilities might be:

7. Imaginative variations on these ideas can make rhythmic dictation a fascinating game. Have a student clap a rhythm and the entire class "say" the rhythm in response. Instead of clapping, try playing the rhythm on one note or by repeating one chord.

RHYTHM EXERCISES (Students' Manual page 10)

The students are directed to tap and say these rhythms. The students should take a breath when the apostrophe (breath sign) appears:

MORE CHALLENGING RHYTHM PROJECTS

The following projects do not appear in the Students' Manual and the patterns must be written on the blackboard.

1. Direct the class to try two rhythm jobs at the same time by clapping the upper rhythm pattern and "walking" the lower:

2. Using the preceding pattern again, the class should say all the "tah" notes but clap the "tee" notes.
3. Direct the class to "walk" all "tah" notes and tap all "tee" notes in this same pattern.
4. Using one of the patterns from the rhythm exercises, ask the class to tap the "tah" notes with the left hand and the "tee" notes with a pencil in the right hand.

ASSIGNMENT (Students' Manual page 10)

1. Clap and say the Rhythm Exercises a) and b). Then walk (in place) evenly while clapping and saying them.
2. Tap Rhythm Exercises c) and d) with your right hand and beat the walking rhythm evenly with your left hand on your desk or knee.
3. Write three rhythm exercises of your own (not longer than the ones in Unit One) and practice clapping and saying them.
4. Practice the Singing Exercises while using hand signals.
5. Write three short melodies using S and M. Be able to sing them with hand signals.

(Space and staves are provided in Students' Manuals for assignments at the end of each unit.)

FURTHER SUGGESTIONS FOR MELODIC ACTIVITIES

Hand Signals

1. The teacher builds simple melodies by making a succession of hand signals which the class imitates as they sing the syllables. The teacher must always sing the starting pitch.
2. One student shows hand signals to the class. The rest of the class imitates the hand signal and sings the syllables.
3. The teacher sings syllables *without* hand signals. The students sing them back *with* hand signals.

Syllables

1. Having established a pitch, the teacher points to a syllable on the board. Half of the class is assigned to sing only when the So is pointed to. The other half of the class sings only when the Mi is pointed to.
2. Divide the class into two sections. By showing the hand signals to one section, that group is led to sing a "question" (half of a musical sentence). Then the other half of the class is shown the answering signals. For example:

First section is shown the signals for: **2** | | | ⊓ | ‖
      S M S M S

Second section is shown the signals for: **2** | ⊓ | | 𝄽 ‖
      S M M S

29

Ear Training

1. The teacher points to a syllable letter on the board. These should be written

to show that **So** is higher than **Mi.** Point out patterns such as "**S M M S**" as the students watch. They memorize what has been pointed to, and sing back with hand signals.
2. The teacher gives two, three or four hand signals to the class. They watch and memorize, then sing the syllables for the entire pattern.
3. The teacher plays or hums two, three, or four note patterns. A volunteer student can be asked to sing it back with syllables and hand signals.

"Live Piano"

A single student (or group of students) is selected to represent one syllable. The teacher improvises melodies by pointing to the individuals (or sections) who sing only their *own* syllable.

Dictation

Different colored pencils or colored chalk may be used to represent different syllables. For instance, **So** can be written with *red*, while **Mi** is written in *blue*.

Unit Two

Pitch Presentation

ROTE SONG

Teach this new song (refer to Students' Manual, page 11).

HUMILITY

Words by Robert Herrick

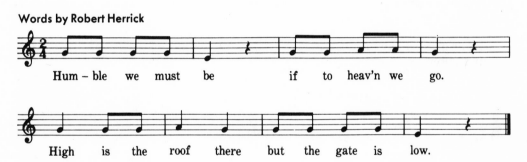

Hum – ble we must be   if to heav'n we go.

High is the roof there but the gate is low.

1. When the students have learned the song they should determine the syllables for each tone. They should first agree that all the tones are **So** and **Mi** except for the words "heav'n we" and the word "roof." The teacher can help the students to recognize the **So-Mi** by first singing, then humming, "Humble we must be" and "but the gate is low." Or the teacher may simply hum the sounds of **So-Mi.** Point out that when the class sang the words "Heav'n" and "roof" they went higher than the sound of **So.** This new sound which is one tone higher than **So** can now be identified as **La.**
2. Direct the class to sing the tones **So-La-So.** The melodic tendency of the sound **La** is toward the **So.** This relationship should be emphasized by pointing out how smoothly the **La** melts into the **So.**
3. The hand signals express the **La** moving to **So,** the loose hand falling smoothly and naturally into the **So** position. Teach the **La** hand signal and have the class sing **So-La-So** with hand signals so that the students may feel the relationship. These positions are shown in their manuals.

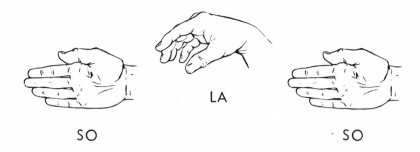

LA

SO   SO

After learning "Humility," the students should use hand signals while singing with syllables. The syllables and signals appear in the Students' Manual page 12.

SINGING DRILLS (Students' Manual page 13)

1. The students are directed to use hand signals while singing the drills slowly:

a) S M S L S M S	e) L L S M L M L
b) S L S M S L S	f) M L L S L M M
c) S L L S M M S	g) M L S L S M S
d) S M M S L M M	h) S L M M S M M

2. Ask the class if they recognize "So-La-So" in songs which begin with these sounds. For example:

SILENT NGHT

S   L   S   M

Si – lent   night

CAMPTOWN RACES

S   S   M   S   L   S   M

Camp-town la – dies   sing this song

3. Have them suggest other songs which begin with "So-La".

SUGGESTIONS: RHYTHM

1. Direct the class to sing "Humility" (with words rather than syllables) and to clap the rhythm as they sing.
2. To enforce the idea that music contains a recurrent accent (pulse), the teacher might sing "Humility" to the class in the following *two* ways. The class is to determine which way sounds correct:

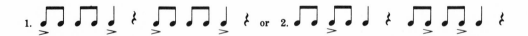

A humorous effect may be obtained if the teacher grotesquely overemphasizes the accents of the second. Now is the time to point out that accents in the correct places for both words and music make the song sound natural.

3. To recognize these important accented beats the song is divided with *bar lines*. (The bar line is a visual aid which should be explained as an accent or pressure mark which is placed in front of the important accented note). Ask the class to find how many beats there are from one bar line to the next. They will see there are two beats in each section between bar lines; these are called *measures*. Point out that the bar line is not needed before the first note in a composition:

$$2 \quad \cap \ \cap \Big|\overset{|}{\underset{\text{S S S }\ \ \text{M}}{}} \ \ \invamp \ \ \Big|\cap \ \cap \Big|\overset{|}{\underset{\text{S S L L }\ \text{S}}{}} \ \ \invamp \ \ \Big|$$

4. The class should sing "Humility" again while tapping two beats in every measure. In the last measure the class should have sung the "Mi" on the first beat, but should only have tapped on the second beat (there *is* no note to sing). They have "rested" their voices. The symbol for that rest which represents the "tah" is then presented to them ($\invamp$). Especially for the benefit of those students who take instrumental lessons the teacher can point out that:

tah note $\quad | \quad = \quad \downarrow \quad$ quarter note

tee notes $\quad \cap = \quad \sqcap \quad$ eight notes

tah rest $\quad \invamp \quad = \quad \invamp \quad$ quarter rest

The number "2" which is shown before the song is really marked $\frac{2}{4}$ Time.

Conducting

A composition can be performed more smoothly if the rhythm is conducted. More flow can be obtained by conducting than by the device of tapping. Teach the conducting pattern for Two-Beat Time.

The strongest beat in any measure is always the first beat. The strongest motion of the arm is *down*. Therefore the first beat of the conducting pattern is a downward motion.

The basic pattern for duple time is:

33

When the students can do it comfortably, the movement can be made more smoothly like this:

The class should now sing "Humility," first with words and then with the syllables *while conducting*. A conducting plan for "Humility" will be found in the Students' Manual page 14.

CONDUCTING PLAN FOR "HUMILITY"

1.

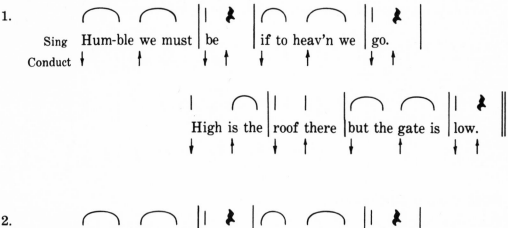

2.

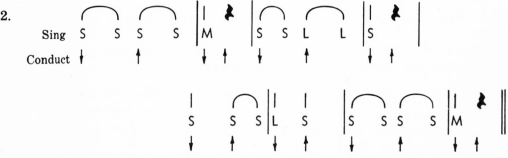

Have the class say the rhythm of "Humility" while conducting. When the rest sign (𝄾) appears, the word "rest" must be said. This will be found in the Students' Manual page 14. Explain that the numeral 2 preceding the line indicates "Two-Beat Time."

34

3.

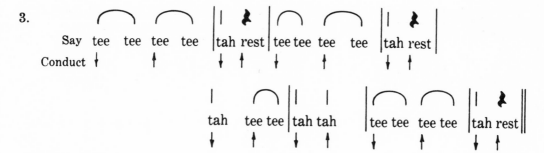

Say tee tee tee tee | tah rest | tee tee tee tee | tah rest |
Conduct ↓ ↑ ↓ ↑ ↓ ↑ ↓ ↑

tah | tee tee | tah tah | tee tee tee tee | tah rest ‖
↓ ↑ ↓ ↑ ↓ ↑ ↓ ↑

RHYTHM EXERCISES

These exercises appear in the Students' Manual page 14. Each exercise should first be tapped and said, then conducted and said:

a) 𝟤 | ∩ | | | | ∩ | | | | | ' | ∩ ∩ | | | | | ∩ | | | ‖

b) 𝟤 ∩ | | ∩ ∩ | | ∩ | | | ' | ∩ | | ∩ | | ∩ ∩ | | 𝄽 ‖

c) 𝟤 ∩ ∩ | | | | | ∩ | | 𝄽 ' | ∩ | | ∩ | | | ∩ | | 𝄽 ‖

d) 𝟤 | | | ∩ ∩ | | ∩ | | 𝄽 ' | | ∩ | | ∩ | 𝄽 ∩ | | 𝄽 ‖

e) 𝟤 ∩ | | 𝄽 | | ∩ ∩ | | | ' | ∩ | | ∩ ∩ | | ∩ | 𝄽 | ‖

MORE CHALLENGING RHYTHM PROJECTS

These exercises do not appear in the Students' Manual and must be written on the board:

1. Divide the class into two sections to perform the following exercises. Each group should first do their part separately:

a)

1st Group Taps — | | | ∩ | | | ∩ | | ' | ∩ | | ∩ | | | ∩ | | ‖

𝟤

2nd Group Claps — ∩ ∩ | | | | ∩ ∩ | ∩ | ' | ∩ ∩ | | | | ∩ | | | | ‖

b)

1st Group Claps — | ∩ | | | | ∩ ∩ | | | ' | ∩ | | ∩ ∩ | | ∩ | | 𝄽 ‖

𝟤

2nd Group Taps — | | | ∩ | | ∩ | | | 𝄽 | | ∩ | ∩ | | ∩ ∩ | | 𝄽 ‖

2. The class performs the following rhythms by tapping all "tah" and "tee" notes on the desk with the right hand and slapping the knee on all rests:

a)

b) 2 ∩ ∩ | I 𝄽 | ∩ I | ∩ ∩ | 𝄽 ∩ | I I | ∩ 𝄽 | 𝄽 I ‖

3. Conduct the time with the left hand and tap the rhythm with the right hand on the desk:

Right Hand I I | ∩ I | ∩ ∩ | I 𝄽 | ∩ I | ∩ I | I ∩ | I 𝄽 ‖
2
Left Hand ↓ ↑ | ↓ ↑ | ↓ ↑ | ↓ ↑ | ↓ ↑ | ↓ ↑ | ↓ ↑ | ↓ ↑ ‖

SINGING EXERCISES

The following Singing Exercises, which combine melody and rhythm, will be found in the Students' Manual page 15. Each exercise must first be tapped and said to secure its rhythm, and then sung with hand signals:

a) 2 I I | I I | ∩ I | I 𝄽 | I I | I I | ∩ I | I 𝄽 ‖
S S | M S | L L S | S | L L | S M | S S M | M

b) 2 I ∩ | I I | ∩ I | I I' | ∩ I | I I | ∩ I | I 𝄽 ‖
S S S | L S | S S M | S S | L L S | M S | L L S | S

c) 2 I ∩ | I I | I I | I 𝄽 | I ∩ | I I | I I | I 𝄽 ‖
S L L | S M | L L | S | L L L | S M | M S | M

d) 2 I I | I I | ∩ I | I I' | ∩ I | I I | ∩ I | I I ‖
M M | S S | L L S | L M | L L S | M S | L L S | M M

e) 2 ∩ ∩ | I I | ∩ ∩ | I I' | ∩ ∩ | I I | I ∩ | I 𝄽 ‖
S S M S | M M | S S L S | M M | L L S M | M L | S | L L M

f) 2 ∩ ∩ | I I | ∩ ∩ | I I' | ∩ I | ∩ I | ∩ ∩ | I I ‖
S M M L | M M | L L S L | M M | M M L | S L M | L S M M | M M

36

SUGGESTIONS: MELODIC DICTATION PROCEDURES

1. a) The teacher sings on a neutral syllable or hums a melody of three or four notes. (All melodies should begin with either **S M** or **S L**. For example: **S L S S; S M S S; S L S M S**)
   b) The class sings or hums it back.
   c) An individual, or entire class, sings it back with syllables and hand signals.
   d) Class writes it down with syllables.
2. a) The teacher plays three or four notes on an instrument.
   b) Volunteers sing back the patterns with syllables.
3. a) A student comes before the class and shows various hand signals slowly.
   b) The class writes down the syllable names, then sings them.

ASSIGNMENT (Students' Manual page 16)

1. Practice the rhythm and melody exercises of Unit 2.
2. Practice Rhythm Exercises a) and b) with two hands — the right hand taps the top part with a pencil, and the left hand taps the lower part.
3. Write an original melody for Rhythm Exercise a) using only **So** and **La**. To do this, place the letter **S** or **L** under each note of the rhythm. Be able to sing your melody with hand signals.
4. Following the instructions from No. 3 (above) write a melody for Rhythm Exercise b) using only **So** and **Mi**.
5. Practice Singing Exercises a) and b) while conducting the time.

SUPPLEMENTARY MATERIALS

Rhythm Dictation

The teacher claps a rhythm, or plays it on a single repeated note or chord on the piano. The students clap it back, then write the rhythm. To be certain that the students realize the rests, the teacher should hold his hands apart to indicate the rest when clapping, or lift his hands visibly from the keyboard if playing. Try these rhythms for a start; make up others according to the progress of the class.

a) | ∩ | | | g) ∩ ∩ | | |

b) | | | | ∩ | h) | | | | ∩ ∩

c) ∩ | | ∩ | i) ∩ | | 𝄾 |

d) | ∩ | | ∩   j) ∩ 𝄾 | | |

e) ∩ | | | ∩   k) ∩ ∩ | 𝄾 ∩

f) | ∩ | ∩ | l) | 𝄾 | 𝄾 |

Unit Three

Pitch Presentation

Introduce this unit by singing the "Star Spangled Banner."

STAR-SPANGLED BANNER

Francis Scott Key   John Stafford Smith

38

1. Direct the class to sing only the first two words ("O say") of the National Anthem with "lah."

   a) Have the class determine how many notes were sung to those first two words: (Answer: Three)

   b) The class should hum the first two notes to determine whether the second note is higher or lower than the first.

   c) Follow the same procedure to determine whether the third note is higher or lower than the second.

2. The teacher hums the first two notes while the class determines the corresponding syllables (**So and Mi**).

   a) It should now be pointed out that the third note is not only lower but stronger than the others. This note, called **Do,** is like a magnet to which the other notes are pulled.

   b) Have the class sing the tones **So-Mi-Do** so that they may experience the strength and firmness of the **Do**:

   c) This new note must be expressed by a very strong motion. Teach the new hand signal; it is shown in their books.

   DO

PITCH DRILLS (Students' Manual page 17)

The students are directed to sing these drills slowly with hand signals. The teacher should precede these drills by playing **S M D** in C Major or in other keys suitable for the students' vocal range.

a) S M S M D

b) S S M S M D D

c) S M S M M M D

d) D D S S M S D

e) M S M D M S S

f) S M S S D D D

g) D D S M S L S

h) S L S M S M D

i) S M D M S L S

j) M S L S M S D

AURAL DICTATION

Hum or play on the piano short (three or four note) melodies. Volunteers from the class say the names of the syllables and the entire class then sings the pattern with syllables and hand signals.

Possible melodic patterns are:

S M D; D M S; S M S D; D D S M; M S M D; S L S D

ROTE SONG

Teach the new rote song, "Jack Be Nimble" (refer to Students' Manual, page 18).

JACK BE NIMBLE

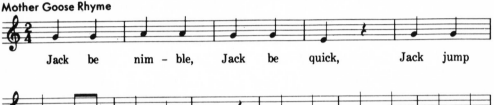

Mother Goose Rhyme

Jack   be   nim – ble,   Jack   be   quick,   Jack   jump

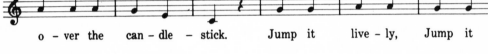

o – ver the   can – dle – stick.   Jump it   live – ly,   Jump it

quick, But   don't knock   o – ver the   can – dle – stick.

1. After the song has been learned, the teacher may hum four measure units. The students should discover the syllable names for the tones of the song.
2. Use "Jack Be Nimble" in ways we have discussed in this and previous units. Discover some new ways to teach the elements of the song.

SUGGESTIONS: PROCEDURES FOR RHYTHMIC-MELODIC DICTATION

From this unit on, the students are directed to write the "tee" (eighth) notes in this manner (⊓) which is closer to the actual music notation. Space is provided in the students' manuals for writing dictation exercises.

1. The teacher plays or hums this melody:

$$2 \quad \begin{matrix} \text{♩} & \text{♫} & | & \text{♩} & \text{♩} \\ \text{S} & \text{M D} & | & \text{S} & \text{S} \end{matrix}$$

2. The pupils first clap the rhythm and write it:

40

3. The teacher plays the melody again while the students recognize the melodic pattern and sing the syllables.
4. The students then write the syllable letters below the rhythm notes, placing the long notes below the **tah's** and the short notes below the **tee's**:

$$| \; \sqcap \; | \; |$$
S MDS S

5. Finally, the students divide the pattern into two-beat timing thus making two measures:

2 | ⊓| | ‖
S MD|S S ‖

6. Other patterns can be dictated in the same way. Possible melodies might be:

2 | | |⊓ | ‖| | |⊓ | ‖| | |⊓ | ‖
S M |S M D ‖D M |S S M ‖S L |S M D ‖ etc.

SINGING EXERCISES (Students' Manual page 19)

1. The students are instructed to first tap the rhythm of each melody and then sing in rhythm with hand signals:

a) **2** | | || | || | || 𝄾 || ⊓|| | || | || 𝄾 ‖
S S |M D |S L |S   L L|S M |D D |D   ‖

b) **2** | ⊓|| | || | || 𝄾 || ⊓|| | || | || 𝄾 ‖
S MM|S M |D M |S   S LL|S M |S S |D   ‖

c) **2** | | || | || ⊓ || 𝄾 || | |⊓ | || | || 𝄾 ‖
D D |S L |S MM |S   L S |MMD |L S |D   ‖

d) **2** | ⊓|| ⊓|| | || 𝄾 |⊓ | |⊓ | || ⊓|| 𝄾 ‖
S MD|S MD|S L |S   S S M |S S D |M SM|D   ‖

e) **2** | ⊓|| | || | || 𝄾 |⊓ | |⊓ | || | || 𝄾 ‖
D DD|S M |D S |S   MM S |MM D |S L |S   ‖

f) **2** | ⊓|| | || | || 𝄾 || | |⊓ | || | || 𝄾 ‖
S LL|S D |S M |S   M S |LL S |M D |D   ‖

41

2. The following is to be sung with hand signals and then conducted while singing without hand signals:

Placing the Syllables on the Staff

1. Explain that music is written on a group of lines and spaces called a "staff." Although the instrumental students will know that such a staff has five lines, the syllables which the class knows can fit on a *three* line staff.
2. The following relationships of syllables on the three line staff must be presented to the students. The class can write them in their manual page 20:
   a) When **So** is a *line* note (the line passes through the note) then **Mi** and **Do** are written on the next lines below:

   b) When **So** is a *space* note (the note is above or below a line) then **Mi** and **Do** are written in the next spaces below:

   c) **La** is one note higher than **So**, and therefore, when **So** is a line note, **La** is written on the next *space* higher:

   And when **So** is a space note, **La** is on the next *line* above:

3. Assist the class in putting the first Singing Exercise on the three line staff. The first four notes can be written on the board for the students to copy and discuss. The class should then continue with the rest of the melody. The rhythm to be written above the notes:

42

4. Place the following melody on the board. The class should sing with hand signals. Then one group sings while conducting as the other group claps the beats (two per measure) and sings:

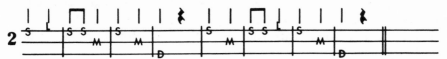

5. The class should place "Jack Be Nimble" on the three line staff (Students' Manual page 20).

RHYTHM EXERCISES (Students' Manual page 20)

1. Tap these rhythms with your right hand and *say* the counting:

a) Tap 2 | ⊓ | | | | ⊓ ⊓ | | ⅋ | ⊓ | | ⊓ ⊓ | | ⊓ | | ⅋ ‖
   Say   1 2 | 1 2 | 1   2 | 1   2 | 1   2 | 1 2 | 1 2 | 1   2 ‖

b) 2 | | | ⊓ | | | ⊓ | | | '| ⅋ | | ⅋ | | ⊓ ⊓ | ⅋ | ‖

c) 2 ⊓ ⊓ | | | | ⅋ ⊓ | | ⅋ | ⊓ | | ⊓ ⊓ | ⅋ ⊓ | | | ‖

d) 2 | ⊓ | | ⅋ | ⊓ ⅋ | | | | ⅋ ⊓ | ⅋ | | | ⊓ | ⅋ | ‖

2. Sing the following rhythm exercises on the note **So** and beat (or conduct) the time — two per measure.

a) 2 | | | | ⊓ | ⊓ | | | ⅋ | | ⊓ | ⊓ ⊓ | | ⅋ | | ⅋ ‖

b) 2 ⊓ | | ⅋ ⊓ | ⊓ ⊓ | | | '| ⅋ ⊓ | ⊓ | | ⊓ ⊓ | ⅋ | ‖

3. Group Exercise — Group One beats the time and says the rhythm while Group Two claps the rhythm:

Group One 2 | ⊓ | ⊓ | | | ⅋ ⊓ | | | ⊓ | | ⅋ ‖

Group Two 2 | | | ⅋ ⊓ | | ⅋ | ⊓ | | ⊓ | ⅋ |

43

1. Practice the Rhythm Exercises by saying the rhythms and conducting the time.
2. a. Write Singing Exercises a), b), and c) on the three line staff using **So** in the space between the second and third lines.
   b. Write Singing Exercises d) and e) on the three line staff using **So** on the top (third) line.
3. Memorize "Jack Be Nimble" with syllables and hand signals.
4. Compose melodies using **So, Mi, Do** below the Rhythm Exercises in No. 2.

Space is provided in the students' manual for additional class work. Repeat some of the more difficult examples and add new ideas of your own to stimulate class participation.

Unit Four

Pitch Presentation

Direct the class to sing part of "The Camptown Races" as an introduction to this unit. Refer to Unit One for this entire song.

The Camp-town la – dies   sing   this   song :   Doo-dah !   Doo-dah !   The

Camp-town   race   track   five   miles   long,   Oh,   doo – dah   day !

1. When the class has sung the song, attention should be focused upon the last three notes:

(Oh,)   doo – dah   day !

The class must be encouraged to find the syllables (through the use of hand signals) for these notes. "Re" is the note between **Do** and **Mi**.

2. Teach the **Re** hand signal as an expression of the bridge between **Do** and **Mi**. These are shown in the students' book, page 22.

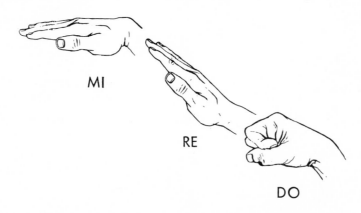

MI

RE

DO

PITCH DRILLS (Students' Manual page 22)

Do can be any tone from B to F sharp. The drills are to be sung with hand signals:

a) M R D

b) D R M

c) D R M R D R M

d) M M R D R R M

e) D R R M M R D

f) M M M R D M M

g) D M M R D M D

h) D M R R M M D

i) S M M R M S S

j) S S M R D R M

k) M R R M S M S

l) M R M S D R D

SUGGESTION: "THE LIVE INSTRUMENT" PROJECT

1. Choose four students of varying heights. The tallest child is to be **Do,** the next to the tallest is **Re,** the next smaller child is **Mi,** the very smallest child is **So.** Note that this arrangement is similar to the pipe system of an organ — the longest pipe (child) produces the lowest sound, etc.
2. The teacher sings with a neutral syllable short three or four note melodies. (They can also be played on the piano.)
3. One volunteer sings back the entire pattern and then the entire group sings it back with hand signals.
4. The "live instrument" then sings it back — each child sings only his assigned note of the pattern.
5. The following are sample patterns to be performed first by the class and then by the "live instrument."

a) S M R D

b) D R M D

c) D R M S

d) S M R M

e) M R M D

f) D M R M

g) M S D R M

h) M D M R D

ROTE SONG

Here is another song for the class to learn, making use of all the syllables we have been singing.

CORAL

Words by Christine Rossetti

O sail-or, come a-shore, What have you brought for me?

Red cor-al, white cor-al, Cor-al from the sea.

1. After the class has learned the song it should be sung again in two measure units and the syllables determined. The entire song should then be sung with syllables and hand signals. Special emphasis should be placed upon the **Re** as it leads up from **Do** to **Mi.**

What   have   you   brought   for   me?

and down from **Mi** to **Do.**

Cor – al   from   the   sea.

2. Direct the class to write the syllables under the words of the song (Students' Manual page 23).

The Music Staff

1. The three line staff can be used to write the **Do-Re-Mi.**
   If **Do** and **Mi** are line notes, then **Re** is in the space between:

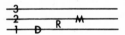

If **Do** and **Mi** are space notes, then **Re** is on the line between:

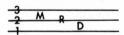

2. The three line staff is no longer sufficient to handle all of the notes now known. Only if **Do** were on the first line could all the notes fit:

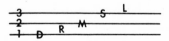

Let the class discover what happens if **Do** is in the first space:

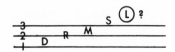

47

The class will see that a fourth line would be needed:

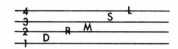

Even the four line staff will not be sufficient if **Do** is placed above the second line.

3. Present the five line staff as the actual music staff:

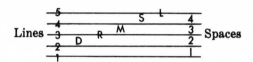

4. Have the students drill placing the syllables on the five line staff as indicated in the Students' Manual page 23.
5. Direct the class to place the song "Coral" on the five line staff (Students' Manual page 24). "So" should be on the on the third space. Additional starting places can also be used.

NOTE VALUES

1. The class should sing "Brother John", this time conducting in Two Beat Time as they sing. Discuss how many conductor's beats are needed on the final word "John."

Broth-er | John

2. The note value which extends over two beats is now presented as two tah notes "tied" together

and then as the half note (♩), which is said:

ta-ah

and conducted:

48

3. When clapping the "ta-ah" (𝅗𝅥), the hands should be held together on the second beat.
4. The rhythm of the rote song can now be determined and written above the notes on the five line staves (Students' Manual page 24).

RHYTHM EXERCISES (Students' Manual page 24)

1. Conduct and say, then clap and say the following rhythms:

a) 2 | | | 𝅗𝅥 | | | | 𝅗𝅥 ' | ⊓ | ⊓ | | | | 𝅗𝅥 ‖

b) 2 | ⊓ | 𝅗𝅥 | | ⊓ | 𝅗𝅥 ' | 𝅗𝅥 | ⊓ | | | | ⊓ | | | ‖

c) 2 𝅗𝅥 | ⊓ | | 𝅗𝅥 | ⊓ | ' | ⊓ ⊓ | | | | 𝅗𝅥 | ⊓ | | ‖

d) 2 | ⊓ | | 𝄽 | 𝅗𝅥 | | 𝄽 | | ⊓ | ⊓ ⊓ | 𝄽 ⊓ | 𝅗𝅥 ‖

2. Tap the rhythm and say the counts while tapping. Say the "One" quite strongly, and the "two" a bit softer:

2 | | | ⊓ ⊓ | | 𝄽 | | | | ⊓ ⊓ | | | | | 𝄽 | ⊓ | ‖

Say   One two | One two | etc.

SINGING EXERCISES (Students' Manual page 24)

a) 2 | | | ⊓ | | | | | 𝅗𝅥 ' | ⊓ | | ⊓ | | | | 𝅗𝅥 ‖
   S M | R R D | S L | S | S M S | S M S | M R | D ‖

b) 2 | | | | | | | | | ⊓ | ' | | ⊓ | | | | | ⊓ | 𝅗𝅥 ‖
   D R | M D | S S | M R D | S L L | S M | S M S | D ‖

c) 2 | ⊓ | | | | ⊓ | 𝅗𝅥 ' | | ⊓ | | | | ⊓ ⊓ | 𝅗𝅥 ‖
   S M S | D R | M R D | R | S M S | D R | M S M R | D ‖

d) 2 | | | 𝅗𝅥 | | | | 𝅗𝅥 ' | | ⊓ | | 𝄽 | | | | 𝅗𝅥 ‖
   M R | D | S L | S | D R R | M | M R | D ‖

e) 2 ⊓ ⊓ | | | | ⊓ ⊓ | 𝅗𝅥 ' | | ⊓ | | | | | ⊓ | 𝅗𝅥 ‖
   M M S L | S | D | D R M M | S | M R D | S S | M M R | D ‖

SUGGESTION: DICTATION PROCEDURE

1. Play or hum a melody. It should contain material used thus far (tones: **L S M R D,** and rhythms:

   and should not exceed two measures.
2. The class sings back the tune with hand signals.
3. They write down the syllable names.
4. Play the tune again, this time calling attention to the rhythm.
5. Now the class claps and recites the rhythm.
6. The students combine this rhythm with the melody by writing it above the proper syllable.
7. Finally they all sing back the entire melody.

ASSIGNMENT (Students' Manual page 25)

1. Learn "Coral" with hand signals and syllables "by heart."
2. Practice Rhythm Exercise d) by saying and conducting the time.
3. Practice Rhythm Exercises a) and b) at the same time by tapping a) with a pencil in the right hand, and b) with the left hand palm tapping on the desk.
4. Compose a melody above any two Rhythm Exercises. Use the syllables we know and end on either **Do** or **So.** Be able to sing what you have written.
5. Put the Singing Exercises on the five line music staff with **Do** either on lines 1 or 2, or in spaces 1 or 2.

Unit Five

Part Singing

HAND SIGNAL REVIEW

Show the hand signals for the following patterns. As each signal is shown, the class repeats the signal and sings the syllable. **So** can be any note from F to A. The teacher should sing the starting note of each pattern and help only when necessary during the rest of each exercise.

a) S M M R D S S

b) S L S M M R D

c) S M M R D D R

d) D R M M R R D

e) D D R M D R M

f) M M S M S M D

g) S S M S M R M D

h) S L S M R M D

TWO-PART SINGING*

Divide the class into two sections. The *first* group is instructed to follow the hand signals made by the teacher's *right* hand while the *second* group follows the hand signals made by the teacher's *left* hand.

The teacher should change signals quite slowly. The students should sing with a light voice while imitating the hand signals.

The long line after a syllable indicates that the group should hold that tone throughout the drill:

a)
| 1st Group | S ———— |
| 2nd Group | S M S |

b)
| 1st Group | S M S |
| 2nd Group | S ———— |

c)
| 1st Group | S ———— |
| 2nd Group | S M D |

d)
| 1st Group | S M D |
| 2nd Group | S ———— |

e)
| 1st Group | D ———— |
| 2nd Group | S M S D |

f)
| 1st Group | S M R D S |
| 2nd Group | S ———— |

*In Unit Five we have the first approach to part singing. By using our hand signals, we can easily control two groups at one time and make the class aware of the pleasure of singing in parts. With ostinato patterns and canons we further their understanding of two-part rhythmic and melodic ideas.

RHYTHM OSTINATO

1. The class is divided into two sections to tap and say the rhythms shown below (Students' Manual page 27). After the class has completed the first exercise the following points should be made:

   a) The class should be made aware that Group Two has repeated a two measure pattern

   | ⌐⌐ | | |

   continuously. Such a repeating pattern is defined as "ostinato."

   b) Teach this sign, ∕⋅ , so that repeating parts need not be written over and over.

EXERCISES (Students' Manual page 27)

1. The class now performs all these exercises.

a) 1st Group **2** | | | ⌐⌐ ⌐⌐ | | 𝄽 | ⌐⌐ | ' ⌐⌐ | | | | ⌐⌐ ⌐⌐ | | 𝄽 ‖
    2nd Group | ⌐⌐ | | | | | ⌐⌐ | | | | | ⌐⌐ | | | | | ⌐⌐ | | | ‖

b) 1st Group **2** ⌐⌐ | | | | | 𝄽 ⌐⌐ | | | ' ⌐⌐ ⌐⌐ | | 𝄽 | | ⌐⌐ | | | ‖
    2nd Group   ⌐⌐ ⌐⌐ | | | | ⁒ | ⁒ | ⁒ ‖

2. The next two Rhythm Exercises are to be tapped and said with this new ostinato pattern:

   ⌐⌐ | | | | |

   The group performing the ostinato should do their part several times before being joined by the other group so that the students will gain confidence and a strong rhythmic swing will be effected.

a) **2** ⌐⌐ ⌐⌐ | | 𝄽 | | ⌐⌐ | | | ' | ⌐⌐ | | ⌐⌐ | | | | ⌐⌐ | | | ‖

b) **2** ⌐⌐ | | ⌐⌐ ⌐⌐ | | ⌐⌐ | | | ' | | 𝄽 | ⌐⌐ | | ⌐⌐ ⌐⌐ | | 𝄽 ‖

3. Sing "Coral" and clap this ostinato pattern to it while you sing:

   | | | ⌐⌐ | |

RHYTHM CANON

Divide the class into two sections to tap and say the following rhythm exercises. After the first exercise has been completed it must be pointed out that the

52

second group has sung exactly the same part as the first group but begins singing it later. Such an "imitating" composition is defined as a "canon." The numbered entrances must be explained before the rest of the exercises are done.

EXERCISES (Students' Manual page 28)

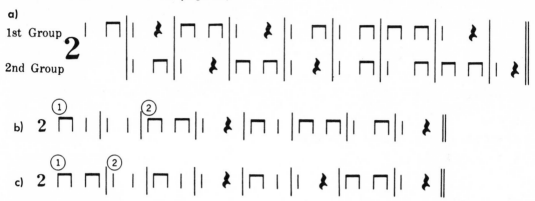

SINGING CANONS

1. Sing the following song (by rote) or any other familiar canon:

WHITE AND GREY SAND

White sand and grey sand. Who'll buy my

grey sand? Who'll buy my white sand?

2. As in the Rhythm Canons, the first exercise has both parts written out. The second one uses the numbered entrances (Students' Manual page 28).

Notation

1. The class is instructed to sing the melody below (Students' Manual page 29):

It should be pointed out that this melody can easily be written in notes, a combination of the rhythm and the syllables.

2. The following essentials of music notation are then discussed (Students' Manual page 29). Here is the place to introduce simple notation, — the use of notes on a staff.

● or ○ = note head

| ⊓ = stem

 line notes (the line passes through the note head)

space notes (the note head is between the lines)

3. When notes are below the third line, the stems are on the right side pointing up:

4. When notes are above the third line, the stems are on the left side pointing down:

5. The note on the third line may have the stem either way:

6. Have the class rewrite the melody in No. 1 with actual notation (Students' Manual page 29).

54

7. The concept of proper music notation can be strengthened by asking the class to criticize the following and/or similar examples which are written on the board:

ASSIGNMENT (Students' Manual page 30)

1. Write the following melody on the staff with notes. **Do** is on the first line.

2. Compose a melody to Rhythm Canon Exercise c). Use **D, R, M, S,** and **L.** Put on the staff with music notes. **Do** is in the first space.
3. Practice singing "Coral" while tapping

ostinato.
4. Practice tapping Rhythm Exercise (Canon) a) with right hand on the upper part, and the left hand doing the ostinato.
5. Write an original melody using **S, M,** and **D** for Rhythm Canon Exercise a).

Unit Six

ROTE SONG

Teach the new song, "Who Has Seen the Wind?"

WHO HAS SEEN THE WIND?

Words by Christine Rossetti

Who has seen the wind? Nei – ther I nor you. But
Who has seen the wind? Nei – ther you nor I. But

when the leaves hang trem – bling, the wind is pass – ing through.
when the trees bow down their heads the wind is pass – ing by.

SUGGESTED PROCEDURES: PITCH

1. Direct the class to sing only,

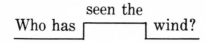

The teacher tells that the starting note is So, the students must discover the rest of the syllables **(S S L L S).**

2. The class now sings,

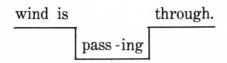

In determining these syllables the student will find that all the words except "passing" are the sound of **Do,** and that "passing" sounds lower than the **Do.**

56

3. Have the class compare the sound of the words **"seen** the" with the word "passing." Half of the class can sing from the beginning through the word "the" and hold that tone while the other half of the class sings the next to the last measure (wind is passing) and holds that tone:

Group One   Who has   seen the

Group Two   wind is   pass-ing

4. The class will discover that the sounds are the same — a high **La** and a low **La**. Low **La** will be written (**L,**). The hand signal is the same as for the higher **La**, but is made below the **Do** hand signal.

PITCH EXERCISES (Students' Manual page 31)

Sing the following drills with hand signals (**Do** may be any tone from D to F):

a) D R M M R D L, L, D   g) D R M S L L S M R M L,

b) D L, D R M M R D L,   h) L, L, D R M S L L L,

c) L, D R M M M L,   i) L S M M S L L

d) L, M M R M R L, L,   j) L L S M R M L,

e) M M R M D L, L,   k) L, L S M S L L,

f) L, M R D L, D D   l) L S M R D L,

PITCH AND RHYTHM EXERCISES (Students' Manual page 32)

In these exercises the following instructions should be observed:

For a) and b),

1. Tap the rhythm and say the syllables (instead of singing them).
2. Then sing the drills with hand signals while maintaining a good smooth rhythm.
3. Lastly, conduct the time while singing.

For c), divide the class with Group Two tapping the ostinato below the melody.

c) Group One
2 𝅗𝅥 D | | | | | | 𝅗𝅥' | 𝅗𝅥 | | | | 𝅗𝅥 | 𝅗𝅥
   R M R D L, M R D L, L,

Group Two | ⊓ | | | | | ⊓ | | | | | ⊓ | | | | | ⊓ | | |

SINGING EXERCISES (Students' Manual page 32)

a) **2** | ⊓ | | | | | ⊓ | | | ' | ⊓ | | | | | ⊓ | | ⁊ ‖
   M R R D D D R M M L, L, M M R D L, D R R L,

b) **2** | | | ⊓ | | | | ⊓ | ' ⊓ ⊓ | | | | | | ⊓ | ‖
   D R D L, L, M R D R M M M S S L M R M L, L, L,

c) **2** | ⊓ | | | | | ⊓ | | | ' | ⊓ | | | | | | | | ⁊ ‖
   L S S M R D R R D L, L S S M R D R L,

d) **2** ⊓ ⊓ | ⊓ | | | ⁊ | ⊓ ⊓ | ⊓ | | | ⁊ |
   M M L L M R L, L, L L S S M M R D

   ⊓ ⊓ | ⊓ | | | ⁊ | ⊓ ⊓ | ⊓ | | | ⁊ ‖
   L L S S M M R M M M L L M R L, L,

e) **2** ⊓ ⊓ | ⊓ | | ⊓ ⊓ | ⊓ | | ⊓ | | ⊓ | | ⊓ ⊓ | ⊓ | ‖
   D D R R M M S L L S M R D L, M R D L, L, M R R D R M L, L,

SUGGESTED PROCEDURES: RHYTHM EXERCISES

1. The teacher must explain that eighth (tee) notes are not only found in pairs (⊓) but can be used separately (⌐ ⌐) as well. If just *one* eighth (tee) note is used, an eighth rest is substituted for the other one. Thus:

   ⌐ ⌐   ⌐ ⁊
   Say tee tee   tee rest

2. The students will need help in the saying of these Rhythm Exercises. During the clapping of rhythms, the hands must not be pulled too far apart during the eighth (tee) rest or they will not be ready in time for the next clap.

3. The teacher might suggest a beginning for Rhythm Exercise No. 3, a) such as:

   2 | | | | ⌐⁊
   S L L S

Exercises No. 3 a) and b) should be sung after the rhythms are completed.

58

RHYTHM EXERCISES (Students' Manual page 32)

1. Divide the class into two groups to tap and say:

2. The first of these can be done as a canon by the two groups; Group Two follows the first group two measures later. Tap and say, then conduct the beats and say:

a) 2 ⊓ ⊓| | | | | ⊓| | ⅋ |⊓ | | | | |⊓ ⊓| | ⅋ ‖

b) 2 ⊓ ⊓| | | |⊓ | ' | ⊓| | | | |⊓ | ' |⊓ ⊓| ⅋ | |⊓ | ‖

c) 2 | ⊓ |⌐ ⅋ | |⊓ ⅋ ⌐| | | ' |⊓ | | ⅋⌐⊓| | ⅋⌐| | | ‖
   tah tee tee | tee rest tah |

d) Group One 2 | | |⊓ ⅋⌐|⌐⅋ | | | ⅋ | ⅋⌐| |⊓ ⅋ |⌐⅋⊓| | | ‖
   Group Two | | |⅋⌐ |
   ostinato

3. Put a rhythm above the following melodies. Use ⌐ and ⅋ and, of course, put in the bar lines: (Students' Manual page 33)

a) **2** S L L S M R M S M D R M R D

b) **2** D R M M R D L, D R R D L, D D

Dictation

SUGGESTED PROCEDURES

1. The teacher claps short rhythms (including ⌐). One student claps it back, and the entire class writes it down. For example,

| | |⅋ ⌐|

2. The teacher hums or plays the following short melodies in rhythm. The class writes the syllables first and then the rhythm above the notes. Tell the students the starting syllable. When each drill has been completed it should be sung with hand signals and then with conducting.

a) **2** | ⊓ || | | ♩ ||
    M R D L, L, L,

b) **2** | | || | ⊓ | 𝄽 ||
    D L, D R R M

c) **2** | | || | ⊓ | 𝄽 ||
    L, L, M R D L,

d) **2** | | | ⊓ | | | 𝄽 ||
    D R M M S D

e) **2** ⊓ | | | ⊓ | | 𝄽 ||
    D R M S L L S

f) **2** ⊓ | | | | | ♩ ||
    M M S M R D

Notation

PLACING LOW "LA" ON THE STAFF

1. Show the relationship of **Do** to the low **La,** both notes being either line notes:

   D L,   D L,   D L,

or both being space notes:

   D L,   D L,   D L,

Let the students practice on the staff in their books.

2. Have the class suggest ways to place "wind is passing through" on the staff. Space has been provided in the Students' Manual page 34. For example:

3. a) Direct the class to place the following melody (Students' Manual page 34) on the staff with notes. **Do** is in the first space.

$$2 \quad \text{D R M} \mid \text{S M R} \mid \text{M R D} \mid \text{L, D} \parallel$$

   b) The students should now try to rewrite the same melody with **Do** placed on the first line. The class will have to be guided into the use of the extra (leger) line needed on the next to last note (the low **La**).
   c) The class is now asked to write "Who Has Seen the Wind?" on the staff with notes. **Do** is to be placed on the first line.

SIGHT SINGING MELODIES (Students' Manual page 35)

1. The class first claps the rhythm.
2. Then they tap the rhythm and say (not sing) the syllables.
3. The students should sing the melodies slowly, using hand signals.
4. Ask the class whether they recognize any of these melodies before they sing them. The first four melodies are rote songs:

Melody a) — "Say Your Name"	(Unit One, Page 8)
Melody b) — "Humility"	(Unit Two, Page 11)
Melody c) — "Jack Be Nimble"	(Unit Three, Page 18)
Melody d) — "Coral"	(Unit Four, Page 23)

a)

b)

ASSIGNMENT (Students' Manual page 36)

1. Sing the melodies of the Pitch and Rhythm Exercises with hand signals while "walking" the beat evenly, in place.
2. "Step" one of the Rhythm Exercises while conducting the time.
3. Make up rhythms to the melodies of the Pitch Exercises. The first one, for example, might begin:

$$2 \quad | \quad | \quad | \sqcap \quad | \quad |$$
$$D \quad R \quad M \; M \; R$$

4. Write melodies a) and b) of the Pitch and Rhythm Exercises on the staff with notes. **Do** is on the second line.
5. Write "Coral" on the staff. **So** will be on the second line.
6. Here is a very challenging task. Sing melody c) of Pitch and Rhythm Exercises while conducting the time with your left hand and tapping the ostinato with your right hand.

62

Unit Seven

The Pentatonic Scale

SUGGESTED PROCEDURES

Instruct the class to sing "Who Has Seen The Wind?" (See Unit Six Rote Song). The teacher writes the syllables on the blackboard, then puts the rhythm above the notes:

$$2 \; \sqcap \; \sqcap \; | \; | \quad \text{\textbf{\textcurrency}} \; | \; \sqcap \; \sqcap \; | \; | \; | \; |$$

S S L L | S | D D R R | M S | etc.

The teacher asks the class to discover how many different notes can be found in the melody. Write the notes which are used starting with the lowest (**L, D R M S L**) or from the highest (**L S M R D L,**).

This scale, which contains *five different* tones, is called a Pentatonic Scale. *Pentatonic* is a combination of two Greek words — *Pente* (five) and *Tonos* (tones). Thus we can say that "Who Has Seen the Wind?" is written in the Pentatonic Scale because it contains five different tones. There is a scale diagram in the Students' Manual.

PENTATONIC EXERCISES (Students' Manual page 37)

a)
| Group One | L, (Hold the La throughout) _____ |
| Group Two | L, L S M R D L, |

b)
| Group One | L, L S M R D L, |
| Group Two | L, _____ |

c)
| Group One | L, _____ |
| Group Two | L, D R M S L L, |

d)
| Group One | L, D R M S L L, |
| Group Two | L, _____ |

If a five note melody ends on **La,** it is probably constructed on the notes of the La Pentatonic Scale.

Sing the following Pentatonic Scales in these rhythms:

e) **2** | ♩ | ♩ ♩ | ♩ | ♩ |
L S M R D L, D R M S L

f) **2** | | | ♩ ♩ | ♩ ♩ | | ♩ |
L, D R M S L S M R D L,

These next two exercises do not appear in the Students' Manual. They are in more difficult rhythms and will provide a challenge for good students:

g) **2** | ♪♩ | ♪♩♩ | | ♩ | ♪♩ | ♩ |
L,   D R M S L S M R D L,

h) **2** ♩ ♪♩ | | ♪♩ | | ♩ | ♪♩ | ♩ |
LS M R D L, D R M S L

Rhythm: Triple Meter

SUGGESTED PROCEDURES

1. Have the class sing the familiar round "Lovely Evening", then clap the rhythm (words) as they sing:

LOVELY EVENING

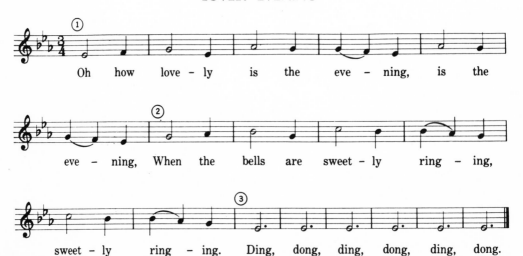

Oh how love - ly is the eve - ning, is the

eve - ning, When the bells are sweet - ly ring - ing,

sweet - ly ring - ing. Ding, dong, ding, dong, ding, dong.

2. The teacher should now instruct the class to clap *only the beats* while again singing the song. They will discover there is a strong pulse followed by two weaker pulses.

As usual, the bar line is placed before each strong pulse, thus giving three beats per measure (Triple Time). The number "3" is shown before such music.

CONDUCTING TRIPLE TIME

1. Teach the basic pattern for Triple Time.

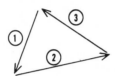

2. When the class can do the basic pattern comfortably, the movement should be smoothed out as follows (this is shown in the students' book):

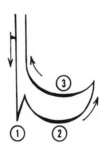

3. The class should now sing "Lovely Evening" while conducting.

4. Teach the note value 𝅗𝅥. from the song, "Lovely Evening." The class can be asked how many beats are used for the words, "Ding, Dong" (Answer: three). In order to show the three beat value, a dot is added to the half note (ta-a-ah). The dot adds one half the value of the preceding note. Three beats can be described as,

$$\textrm{𝅗𝅥} + \textrm{𝅘𝅥} = \textrm{𝅗𝅥.}$$

(Two plus one equals three).

65

RHYTHM EXERCISES (Students' Manual Page 38)

1. Tap the three beats per measure while saying the following rhythms. Then conduct and say them:

a) 𝟑 | | | | ♩ | | | | | ♩ 𝄾 |

  | ♫ ♫ | | | | ♩ ♫ | ♩. ‖

b) 𝟑 ♩ | | | ♫ | | ♩ | | | | | 𝄾 |

  ♫ ♫ ♫ | | | | | | ♫ | ♩ 𝄾 ‖

c) 𝟑 ♫ ♫ ♫ | | ♩ | | ♫ ♫ | ♩ 𝄾 |

  | ♫ | | | ♩ | | ♫ | | ♩ 𝄾 ‖

2. Do the following exercises in two groups. Each group should practice its own part separately until it goes easily. Then both groups perform together.

a)

Group One 𝟐 | | | ♫ | | 𝄾♫♫ | | | ' ♫ | | 𝄾♫ | 𝄾♫♫ | | | ‖

Group Two | ♫ | ♫𝄾 | | ♫ ♫ | 𝄾♫ | ' 𝄾♫♫ | | | ♫ ♫ | 𝄾♫ |

b) Group One claps and Group Two taps the following rhythm canon:

 ① ②
𝟐 ♫ ♫ | | 𝄾 | ♫ 𝄾 | 𝄾♫ | 𝄾 ♫ | ♫ | | 𝄾 ♫ | | | ‖

3. Group One sings the top rhythm on **So** while Group Two sings the bottom rhythm on **Do.**

a)

Group One 𝟐 | | | ♫ ♫ | | | ' | ♫ | | ♫ 𝄾 | | ‖

Group Two | ♫ | | | 𝄾 | ' ♫ | | ♫ | | 𝄾 | |

66

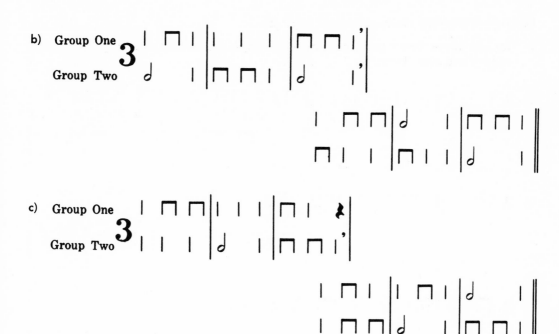

b) Group One / Group Two

c) Group One / Group Two

SIGHT SINGING EXERCISES (Students' Manual page 39)

Sing the following exercises with hand signals. Then conduct and sing:

a) **2** S M R | D R | M R D | R | M M S | L S | M S M R | D ‖

b) **2** D DD | S M | S L | S | L LL | S M | R M | D ‖

c) **2** D R | M M R | D L, D | D R | M M S | M R D | ‖

d) **2** D D | R | D L, D | M M | R | D L, | L, ‖

e) **2** L L L S | M R | M S | L L L S | M R | M M |

R R R D | L, D | R M | R R R D | L, D | L, L, ‖

f) 3 | | ⊓ | | | | ⊓ | | ♩ 𝄽'
L L SS | M R D | M R D L, | D

| | ⊓ | | | | | ⊓ | | ♩ 𝄽 𝄇
R M S S | L L S | M R D L, | L,

g) 3 ⊓ ⊓ ⊓ ⊓ | ♩ | ⊓ ⊓ ⊓ ⊓ | ♩ 𝄽'
L L L L S M | R D | L L L L S M | R

⊓ ⊓ ⊓ | ♩ | ⊓ ⊓ ⊓ ⊓ | ♩ 𝄽 𝄇
M M M M R D | L, D | M M M M R D | L,

h) 3 | | ⊓ | ♩ | | | | ⊓ | ♩ 𝄽
L, L, D R | M S | L L S L | M

| | ⊓ | ♩ | | | | ⊓ | ♩ | 𝄇
L L S L | M R | D R M R | L, L,

SIGHT SINGING MELODIES (Students' Manual page 40)

Perform the melodies in the following ways:
- a) Read the syllable names of the notes.
- b) Clap the rhythm.
- c) Sing with hand signals.
- d) Tap the rhythm while singing without hand signals.
- e) Conduct the time while singing without hand signals.

Dictation

SUGGESTED PROCEDURES

1. The teacher "shows" melodies with hand signals in rhythm.
2. The class waits until the teacher has finished and then they write down the notes (syllable names) first and then the rhythm above the notes; or,
3. They write down the rhythm first and then add the syllables under the rhythm.

Musical Definitions

SUGGESTED PROCEDURES

1. The teacher should choose one of the melodies from Unit Seven and sing it in two ways — the first time softly, the second time loudly.
2. Define "piano" (p) — soft; and "forte" (f) — loud (Students' Manual, page 42).
3. The teacher can now gradually increase the volume of his (her) voice from "piano" to "forte." This presents the concept of the "crescendo" — gradually getting louder. Present the symbol for "crescendo"

The Students' Manual shows the crescendo (pronounced "creh-sheń-doe") as:

4. Have the class sing a crescendo on the note **So.**

5. The teacher should now gradually decrease the volume of his (her) voice to present the concept of the "decrescendo" — gradually getting softer — and its symbol:

The Students' Manual shows the decrescendo (pronounced "deé-creh-shen-doe") as:

6. Have the class sing a decrescendo on the note **So.**

ASSIGNMENT

1. Sing Sight Singing Melodies (1, 2, 3, or 4,) and clap this ostinato to it:

$$2 \mid \quad \mid \mid \sqcap \mid \mid$$

2. Write one melody in Two (Duple) Time and one melody in Three (Triple) Time. Each melody should be four measures long and must use the tones of the Pentatonic scale.

3. Memorize any one melody from either the Sight Singing Exercises or the Sight Singing Melodies with hand signals.

4. Write any two melodies from the Sight Singing Exercises on the staff. **Do** may be either the first space or the second line.

5. Sing the **La Pentatonic** Scale up and down to these rhythms:

a) 2 ♩ | | ⊓ | ♩ | ♩ ‖

b) 2 | | | ⊓ | | ♩ ‖

c) 2 ⊓ | | ♪ | | ⊓ ♪ ‖

70

d) $\mathbf{3}$ | | | | $\vert$ ♩ | | $\vert$ ♩ ⁊ $\Vert$

e) $\mathbf{3}$ ♩ | | $\vert$ | | | | $\vert$ ♩. | $\Vert$

f) $\mathbf{3}$ | ⊓ | $\vert$ ♩ | | $\Vert$

g) $\mathbf{3}$ | ⁊ | $\vert$ | | ⁊ | ♩. | | ♩. | $\Vert$

h) $\mathbf{3}$ | ⁊ | $\vert$ | ⁊ | $\vert$ | ⁊ ⁊ | | ⁊ ⁊ $\Vert$

71

Unit Eight

Pitch Presentation

As an introduction to Unit Eight, have the class sing the first part of "Old Folks at Home."

SUGGESTED PROCEDURE

Ask the class to sing the beginning of "Old Folks at Home":

Have one group hold the first syllable of *"Swa* - nee" while the second group continues to the high second note of the word Swan-*nee."* The class should compare the sound of the low and high notes. The syllables of the section can now be presented. The note at the end is, therefore, the high **Do (D′)**. The class now sings the entire song (not the refrain) with syllables. A diagram of the song has been provided in the Students' Manual page 44, for writing in these syllables.

Ask the class to determine how many different tones are present in the section of "Old Folks at Home" which appears in their manual. They will find the section utilizes the tones of the Pentatonic Scale. Furthermore, the syllable of greatest importance — the highest as well as the lowest tone, and the very last tone of the section is **Do**.

Present the concept of the **Do** Pentatonic Scale (Students' Manual page 45).

PITCH DRILLS (Students' Manual page 45)

a) S M D D' D

b) S D' S M D

c) S M D M S D'

d) D M S D' S S D

e) D D' S M S D' D

f) S L D' L S S D

g) D R M S L D' D

h) D D' L S M M D

SINGING EXERCISES (Students' Manual page 45)

Sing the following melodies with a good, smooth rhythm. Practice with hand signals; then conduct while singing without hand signals:

a) 2 S S S | L L | D' L L | S S | M M S | M M D | R M | D ‖

b) 2 S M R | D S | L D' | S | M M S | L S | M S | D ‖

c) 2 D S | L L S | D' S | M M S | L L D' L | S M | S L D' L | S D ‖

d) 2 D R M S | L L S | D' D' S M | S S | M S L D' | L L S | M M S M | R D ‖

e) 3 S M S | D | D' L D' L | S | S M S | D' | D R R M | D ‖

f) 3 S L S M | D | D' L S L S M | R R |

D D' D' L | S | L S M S M R | D ‖

SUGGESTED PROCEDURES

1. Show the relationship of high **Do (D')** to **La,** both notes being either line notes:

L D'   L D'   L D'

or space notes:

L D'   L D'   L D'

2. Blank staves have been provided for the student. The teacher may suggest syllable patterns for placement on the staff. For example:

 etc.

S M S L D'

3. Show the relationship of high **Do** to the entire **Do** Pentatonic Scale:

D   D' D   D' D   D'

4. The first two measures of Singing Exercise a) are written out for the students in their books. They must complete the melody by placing the notes on the staff.

S S S L L   D' L L   S S   M M S   M M D   R M   D

RHYTHM EXERCISES (Students' Manual page 46)

1.

1st Group Claps

2nd Group Taps

2. Both groups sing the syllables while tapping their separate rhythms. Practice the parts separately before trying them all together:

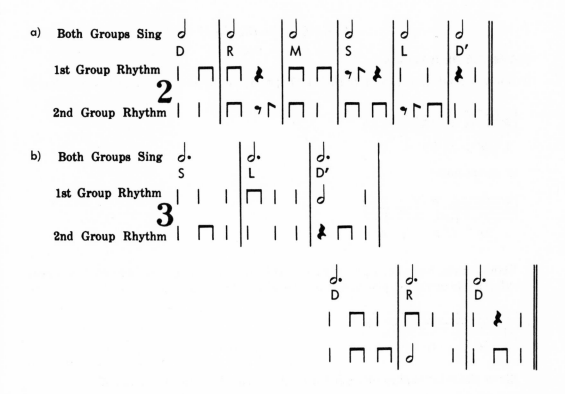

The "Do" Chord (Major Triad)

SUGGESTED PROCEDURES

1. Divide the class into three sections. Following directions from the teacher, these groups enter as follows and hold their respective tones:

a) Group 1   S ———
     Group 2   M ———
     Group 3   D ———

b) Group 1   S ———
     Group 2   M ———
     Group 3   D ———

c) Group 1   S ———
     Group 2   M ———
     Group 3   D ———

Reverse the sections so that *each* group does *each* part.

75

2. Suggest that these three important tones sound pleasantly together. They form a three note chord (Triad). This particular triad is called the **Do** Chord because **Do** is the lowest note.

3. It is easy to recognize this chord on the staff. If **Do** is a line note, so is the entire chord:

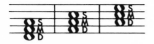

And if **Do** is a space note, so too is the entire chord:

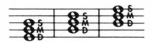

Musical Definition

The term *Mezzo* (medium) should be added to the concepts of *Piano* and *Forte* from Unit Seven. From this point on, expression marks will be used in all Sight Singing Melody Sections. The students should be encouraged to add their own ideas of expression in the Singing Exercises.

SIGHT SINGING MELODIES (Students' Manual page 47)

The signatures of the following melodies are omitted in the Students' Manual.

3.

Dictation

SUGGESTED PROCEDURES

1. The teacher gives the starting note (syllable), then plays two or three measure melodies in Two and Three Time, such as:

a)
2 | | | ⊓ | | | | ||
  D R M M S D D

d)
2 | ⊓ | | | d ||
  S M R D L, D

b)
2 | | | | ⊓ d ||
  M R D L,L, D

e)
3 | ⊓ | | d | d. ||
  D R R M S L S

c)
2 ⊓ | | | ⊓ d ||
  D D L, D R R M

f)
3 | | | d | d. ||
  S L S M S D

a) First one student and then the entire class sings it back.
b) Students first write down the rhythm then the syllables below the rhythm.
c) After the drill has been completed, the entire class should sing through all the melodies.

2. The teacher gives four or five hand signals. The students memorize the entire pattern and then sing it back.

ASSIGNMENT (Students' Manual page 48)

1. Memorize any one of the Singing Exercises with hand signals.
2. Sing the **Do** Pentatonic Scale (one note per measure) while tapping any one of the rhythms in the Rhythm Exercise section.
3. Compose melodies in the **Do** Pentatonic Scale in Two and Three beat Time. The melodies should be eight measures long with a breath at the end of the fourth measure. (The starting note should be **Do** or **So** and the melody should end on **Do**.)
4. Write on the staff any two melodies from the Singing Exercises. **Do** can be either the first line or the first space.

77

Unit Nine

Pitch Presentation

SUGGESTED PROCEDURES

1. *Dictation*

   a) Play the following melody slowly. Instruct the class to decide the syllable name of each tone and sing it just after it has been played. In this way the melody will pull the students along with it. The class is told that the first tone is **Do**.

   D R M R D D L,

   b) Repeat the above procedure but this time the last tone goes one note below the low **La**.
   The note which is one lower than the low **La** is identified as low **So (S,)**.

   D R M R D D L, (S,)

2. The low **So** can be further derived by having the class sing the first four notes of "Bicycle Built for Two."

   Dai - sy,   Dai - sy

   When the class has done this, ask them to hum only the first three and determine their syllables **(S M D)**. Then have them compare the first and fourth tone. This can be easily done by having one group hold the first tone while another group continues singing to the fourth tone. The relationship of **So** and low **So** is the same as that of **La** and low **La**.

3. The first two notes of many Bugle Calls such as "Taps," "Reveille," can also be used to present the sound of **S,-D**.

78

4. Have the class sing the following melody (shown in their books) with hand signals. The signal for low **So** is the same as for the higher **So**, but is made at a much lower level.

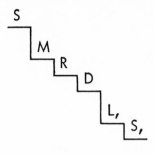

PITCH EXERCISES (Students' Manual page 49)

Note to Teachers: It may be necessary to help by singing along with the class whenever difficulties appear. It is also advisable to have individual students perform these drills as well as the entire class together.

Sing the following with hand signals:

a)   D R M R D L, S, S, D

b)   D L, S, S, D R D

c)   M M R D S, D D

d)   S M R D S, S D

e)   S, S, S M R D D

f)   S, S, D S, L, L, S,

g)   S M S M D S, S,

h)   D R D L, S, S D

SINGING EXERCISES (Students' Manual page 50)

Sing the following melodies and tap the rhythm quietly on your desk:

a) 2 | ⌐ | | | ⌐ | | | 𝄽 | | ⌐ | ⌐ | | | | | | 𝄽 ‖
    D R R M D L, L, S, D   R R R M R D L, S, S,

b) 2 | | | ⌐ | | | | | | | ⌐ | | ⌐ | | ⌐ | | | 𝄽 ‖
    S, D R M D S, D R R M M S M R D L, L, S, D

c) 2 | ⌐ | | ⌐ | | | | | ⌐ | | | | | | | 𝅗𝅥 ‖
    S M D S M D S, S, D D S S M D D S, S, D

d) Can you recognize the following song?

2 𝄐 | | | | | | | | | |' ⌐ | | | | | 𝅗𝅥 |
S, D D D M R D R M R D D M S L

𝄐 | | | | | | | | | ⌐ | | | | 𝅗𝅥 ‖
L S M M D R D R M R D L, L, S, D

e) 2 ⌐ ⌐ | | | | | | | 𝄽 | ⌐ ⌐ | | | ⌐ ⌐ | | 𝄽 ‖
D D D D L, S, D R M S S S S M R D L, S, S, D

f) 2 | ⌐ | | | | ⌐ | | 𝄽 | ⌐ | | | | ⌐ | | | 𝄽 ‖
D R R D L, S, L, L, D D R M R R D L, S, D

g) 3 | ⌐ | | | | | 𝅗𝅥 ⌐ | 𝅗𝅥 𝄽 | | | | | | | | ⌐ | | | 𝅗𝅥. ‖
D D L, S, D R M S L L S M S M R D L, S, S, D R D

h) 3 ⌐ ⌐ | | 𝅗𝅥 | | ⌐ ⌐ | | 𝅗𝅥 𝄽 | | | | | | | | | | 𝅗𝅥. ‖
D R M R D L, S, D R M R D S L D' L S M D R S, S, D

ROTE SONG (For presentation of low So and syncopation)

LI'L LIZA

Traditional American Song

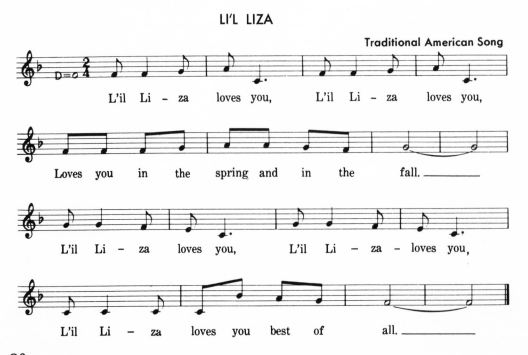

L'il Li - za loves you, L'il Li - za loves you,

Loves you in the spring and in the fall.

L'il Li - za loves you, L'il Li - za - loves you,

L'il Li - za loves you best of all.

After the song has been learned, the concept of the low **So** can be reinforced by having the class discover the syllables for the first four words. The lowest tone on the word "you", as well as that of every other lowest tone is low **So**. Compare the sound of low **La** with that of low **So** by playing or singing the first four words in the following manner:

Then play or sing it again in the correct way, ending on low **So**.

Rhythmic Syncopation

After the class has learned "Li'l Liza," they can be taught the concept of syncopation, which is used in the song.

SUGGESTED PROCEDURES

1. The class sings the song and claps the rhythm as they sing.
2. The students clap and sing only the words "Li'l Li-za".
   The teacher asks how many claps there were. (Answer: "Three")
3. The class is now asked to sing and clap the part, "Loves you best of . . ." The teacher again asks how many claps there were now. (Answer: "Four")
4. The class is now divided into two groups to say the words and clap both of the above measures at the same time:

Group One   L'il   Li   –   za

Group Two   Loves you best of

5. The class now repeats the procedure with only the clapping:

Group One   1   2   4

Group Two   1   2   3   4

At what place did Group Two have to clap alone? (Answer: "On their third clap".)

Point out that Group One had to hold its second clap longer, long enough for Group Two to make its third clap.

6. Now show that both groups have the same rhythm on their first and last notes:

The middle note of Group One is twice as long and is a *tah* (quarter) note against the two *tee* (eighth) notes of Group Two.

7. Show that Group One's long middle note stretches over the second beat of the measure and therefore includes the stress of the second beat. When using the rhythm it is necessary to give an extra stress on the long note in addition to the regular stress of the first note of the measure:

tee tah tee

It is called syncopation. (A diagram in the students' manual shows the conducting pattern for syncopation.)

RHYTHM EXERCISES (Students' Manual page 52)

Clap the beats and say the following rhythms. Then conduct and say them:

Two-Part Exercises

a) Group One Taps
   Group Two Claps

b) Group One Taps
   Group Two Claps

c) Group One Taps
   Group Two Claps

ostinato

d) Group One Taps
   Group Two Claps

RHYTHM-MELODY EXERCISES (Students' Manual page 53)

First practice the rhythm and melody separately. Then work the combined excercises in two groups and with students individually.

SIGHT SINGING MELODIES (Students' Manual page 54)

Perform these melodies in the following ways:
a) Read the syllable names of the notes.
b) Clap the rhythm.
c) Sing with hand signals.
d) Conduct the time and sing without hand signals.

ASSIGNMENT (Students' Manual page 55)

1. Compose melodies containing Low **So (S,)** for the Rhythm Exercises.
2. Learn "Li'l Liza" by heart with words. Clap this ostinato while you sing:

3. Try to clap this more challenging ostinato while singing "Li'l Liza":

$$2 \mid \mid \mid \uparrow \mid \mid \uparrow \mid$$

4. Write Singing Exercise c) on the staff. **Do** is on the second line.
5. Write Singing Exercise g) on the staff. **Do** is in the second space.
6. Practice the Two-Part Rhythm Exercises with two hands — the right hand taps the Group One part while the left hand taps the Group Two part.

Unit Ten

Song Presentation

ROTE SONG

Teach this new rote song as an introduction to Unit Ten. Only the first verse has been printed in the Students' Manual page 57.

FOUR IN A BOAT

Appalachian Mountain Song

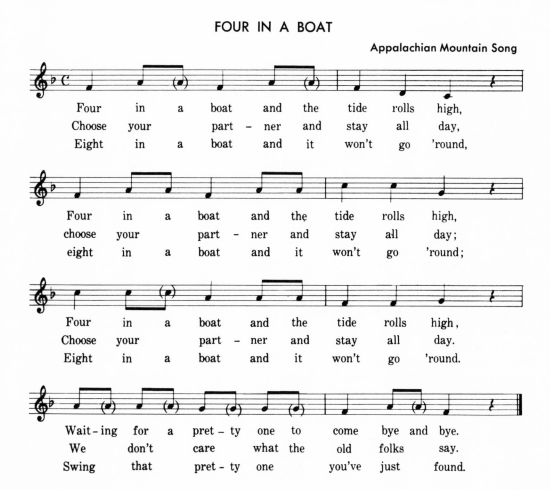

Four in a boat and the tide rolls high,
Choose your part - ner and stay all day,
Eight in a boat and it won't go 'round,

Four in a boat and the tide rolls high,
choose your part - ner and stay all day;
eight in a boat and it won't go 'round;

Four in a boat and the tide rolls high,
Choose your part - ner and stay all day.
Eight in a boat and it won't go 'round.

Wait - ing for a pret - ty one to come bye and bye.
We don't care what the old folks say.
Swing that pret - ty one you've just found.

The "Do" and "La" Chords

SUGGESTED PROCEDURES

1. After the song has been learned, have the class sing only the words "and the tide rolls" as it sounds the *first* time it appears. They should determine the syllables.

2. Compare the sound of "and the tide rolls" with that of the first three notes of "The Star-Spangled Banner" (Use the same key).

3. The three notes

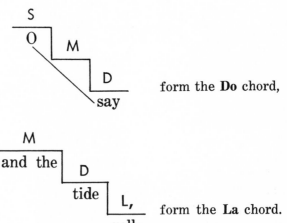

(Hand signals for these chords are shown in the students' book.)

4. Ask the class to describe the difference in the sound of the two chords. For example, the **Do** chord could be described as bright or strong. Its sound is then identified as a *major* chord. The **La** chord might be described as sounding more mild or mellow. Its sound is then identified as a *minor* chord.

5. A further comparison of the major and minor chord sounds can be made by having the class sing the first three notes of "The Star-Spangled Banner" as is

(S-M-D)
Oh—say

and then sing it in *minor*

(M-D-L,)
Oh—say

88

PITCH EXERCISES (Students' Manual page 58)

1. Sing the following **Do** chord drills with hand signals:

a) S M D   c) S M S M D

b) D M S   d) D M D M S

2. Sing the following **La** chord drills with hand signals:

a) M D L,   c) M D M D L,

b) L, D M   d) L, D L, D M

3. Sing with hand signals and compare the following melodies based upon the **Do** (major) chord and the **La** (minor) chord:

a) **Major**

S S M | D D | M S S | D' ' | S D' | S S M | D M | D ‖

b) **Minor**

M M D | L, L, | D M M | L ' | M L | M M D | L, D | L, ‖

Two and Three Part Singing

SUGGESTED PROCEDURES

1. Each group must practice singing its own part slowly and with the best possible intonation before the groups perform the drill together.
2. These drills can also be done by smaller selected groups or by individuals performing in duets and trios.

PART SINGING EXERCISES (Students' Manual page 59)

a) **Group One**

S | S | L | S ' | L L | S | M | S ‖

Group Two

S | M R | D R | M ' | R | M R | D | D ‖

b) **Group One**

D R | M | M S | L ' | L | S | L | L, ‖

Group Two

D R | D L, | M R | D | L, | D R | L, | L, ‖

89

c) **Group One**

$\mathbf{3}$

S	M	D		S	S	S	D′	D′		S	D′ L	D′

Group Two

S	S	S	M	S	D	R	M	M	M D L,	D	R	D

Group One

$\mathbf{2}$

S		L	S	D′.	D′ S	L	L	S	S	D

Group Two

S	M	D		L, D	M	M L	M	D	D	

Group Three

S		M	M	S	D D	L,	D M	D		

Notes on the Staff

SUGGESTED PROCEDURES

1. The **La** and **Do** chords on the staff (Students' Manual page 59).

   a) The **La** chord is found on consecutive lines or spaces as is the **Do** chord. For example,

L,   D   M   D   L,   L,   D   M   D   L,   D   M   S   M   D

   b) This may be the ideal time to define "chord" as being three or more notes placed on adjacent lines or spaces (thus combining intervals of thirds). Further, a "triad" is a three note chord such as the **Do** and **La** chords. (Note the drill work in the students' book.)

2. High **"Re"** and **"Mi"**
   Teach the position of high **Re (R′)** and high **Mi (M′)** on the staff in relation to high **Do (D′)**:

D   R   M   D′   R′   M′   D   R   M   D′   R′   M′

PITCH EXERCISES (Students' Manual page 60)

The following are to be sung with hand signals:

a) S M S L D′ R′ D′   c) M S M D D D′ R′ M′

b) S D′ R′ M′ D′ L S   d) D R M S L D′ R′ M′

e) D′ R′ M′ R′ D′ L S M R D

SIGHT SINGING MELODIES (Students' Manual page 60)

Work the Sight Singing Melodies in the following manner:

    a) Say the syllable names in rhythm.

    b) Sing the melodies with hand signals.

    c) Conduct the melodies while singing without hand signals.

Hungarian Folk Song

Hungarian Folk Song

Dictation

(Space is provided in Students' Manual for taking dictation.)

SUGGESTED PROCEDURES

1. Have the class write the rhythm first and then add the melody (syllable names) underneath the rhythm.
2. The teacher should play (or sing on a neutral syllable) the entire melody once. Then half of the melody should be played. If a four measure phrase is too long a unit to be memorized, dictate just two measures at a time. Each part should be repeated several times in rhythm.
3. The students sing back the syllable names after listening to each section, or they may hum the section so they can individually figure out the syllable names.

The following are suggested dictation melodies:

3. L, D L, D M L' M L' M D M L,

4. D M D M S D S D' S M S D

RHYTHM EXERCISES (refer to Students' Manual page 62)

1. Exercise a)
   a) After the formation of the groups, each group must be rehearsed separately. Group One should sing its rhythm on the pitch **So.** Group Two should sing its rhythm on the pitch **Mi.**
   b) An optional third part is given here which can be added to the regular two parts given in the Students' Manual. This third part is sung on the pitch **Do:**

   Optional
   Third Group 2 | | | 𝄾 | | ⊓ ⊓ | 𝄾 | | | ⊓ | ⌐ | | ⌐ | ⊓ | 𝄾 | 𝄾 | ‖

2. Exercises b) and c)
   The entire class can sing the **La** Pentatonic Scale (used in these Exercises)

   2 𝅗𝅥 | 𝅗𝅥 | 𝅗𝅥 | 𝅗𝅥 | 𝅗𝅥 | 𝅗𝅥 | 𝅗𝅥 | 𝅗𝅥 ‖
     L | S | M | R | D | L, | L | L,

   while tapping the rhythms of Exercise a).

3. Exercise d)
   Divide the class into two groups and tap any of the rhythms in canon. For example, Exercise No. 1 (Group One's Part) could be done as follows:

   ① ②
   2 | ⊓ | 𝄾 | | ⌐ | ⌐ | | 𝄾 etc.

   An interesting addition to the canonic treatment is to have the first group sing their rhythm on the syllable **So** while the following group sings their rhythm on the syllable **Do.** Other interval combinations can be used, of course.

RHYTHM EXERCISES (Students' Manual page 62)

a) Group One 2 | ⊓ 𝄾 | | ⌐ | ⌐ | | 𝄾 | ⊓ ⊓ | | | | ⌐ | ⌐ | | 𝄾 ‖

Group Two | 𝄾 | ⊓ | | 𝄾 ⌐ ⊓ | | | | ⌐ | ⌐ | 𝄾 | 𝄾 ⌐ ⊓ | | | 𝄾 ‖

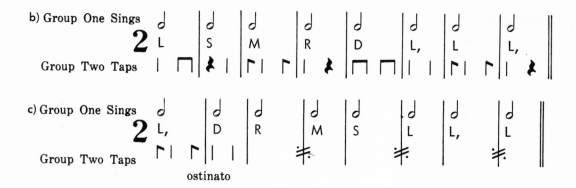

b) Group One Sings / Group Two Taps

2 L   S   M   R   D   L,   L   L,

c) Group One Sings / Group Two Taps

2 L,   D   R   M   S   L   L,   L

ostinato

d) Both groups clap the rhythm canon. Then clap again with Group One sing-ing the rhythm on the syllable **So**, and Group Two singing its rhythm on the syllable **Do**.

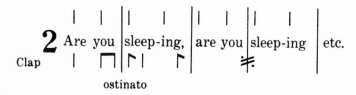

e) Sing the familiar "Brother John" while clapping this ostinato rhythm as you sing:

2 Are you | sleep-ing, | are you | sleep-ing | etc.

Clap

ostinato

(The ostinato part should be clapped twice before the song is begun).

f) Divide into two groups to sing "Brother John" as a two part round and each part claps the ostinato rhythm of e) as you sing:

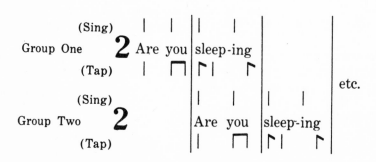

(Sing)

Group One   **2** Are you | sleep-ing

(Tap)

etc.

(Sing)

Group Two   **2** | Are you | sleep-ing

(Tap)

g) Sing and clap the round "Brother John" as in Exercise f), but do it in three parts.

94

ASSIGNMENT (Students' Manual page 63)

1. Memorize any one Sight Singing Melody with hand signals.
2. Practice tapping these rhythms in canon with two hands:

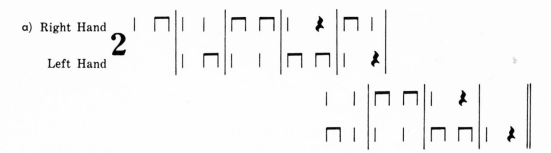

a) Right Hand

Left Hand

b)

3. Sing "Brother John" while tapping these ostinatos:

4 Practice the Sight Singing Melodies without syllables (use hum or neutral syllable).
5. Write Pitch Exercise 3 a) on the staff — **Do** is the first space.
6. Write Pitch Exercise 3 b) on the staff — **Do** is the second line.

Unit Eleven

Song Presentation

ROTE SONG

Teach the new rote song, "Colorado Trail."

COLORADO TRAIL

American Folk Song

Eyes like a morn - ing star, Cheeks like a rose.

Lau - ra was a pret - ty girl, Ev' - ry bo - dy knows.

Weep all ye lit - tle rains. Wail, winds, wail.

All a - long, a - long, a - long the Col - o - rad - o Trail.

Rhythm: Quadruple Meter

SUGGESTED PROCEDURES

1. After the students have learned the "Colorado Trail," direct them to clap the rhythm as they sing.

2. The class now sings the song again, this time clapping only the beats. The song, which is written in quadruple time (4), has one strong pulse followed by three weaker ones. The third beat, however, has a slight stress. Such a rhythmic pulse-pattern may be described as:

3. As usual, the bar line is placed before the strongest pulse thus yielding four beats per measure. The number "4" is shown before such music. It should be also pointed out that the letter "C" is often used in place of the number "4" to represent Four Beat (quadruple) Time.

Conducting Quadruple Time

1. Teach the basic conducting pattern for quadruple time:

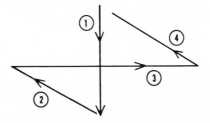

   a) Have the class say "Down-In-Out-Up" while conducting. (By saying "in and out" the left handed student can easily perform the diagram in reverse.)

   b) Have the class say "One-Two-Three-Four" while conducting.

2. When the class can do the basic pattern comfortably, the conducting motion should be smoothed out as follows (diagram shown in students' book):

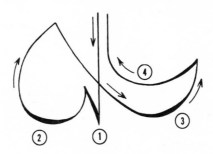

3. The class should practice conducting four-beat measures in the various note values which might comprise a quadruple time measure. The class conducts and "says":

a)   tah   tah   tah   tah | tah   tah   tah   tah

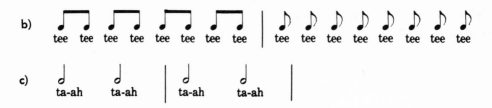

b)

tee tee tee tee tee tee tee tee | tee tee tee tee tee tee tee tee

c)

ta-ah   ta-ah | ta-ah   ta-ah |

4. *New Note Values*

   a) Teach the note value of ○ (whole note):

Count   1 2 3 4

○

Say   ta- a- a- ah

   b) Review the 𝅗𝅥. (dotted half note). It must be explained that the dot is equal to one half of the 𝅗𝅥 (half note) thus extending the length of the 𝅗𝅥 (half note) by an extra beat:

Count   1 2 3 4

𝅗𝅥.   𝄿

Say   ta- a- ah rest

5. As a summary of quadruple time, have the class make up combinations of note values which could be contained in a single measure of Four Beat Time. The class should conduct and say each original pattern. For example:

a)   c)

b)   d)

SUGGESTED PROCEDURES: RHYTHM

1. Have the class sing "Colorado Trail" while conducting the time.

2. Each of the Rhythm Exercises can be performed by two groups. One group conducts and says the count, "One-Two-Three-Four"; the other group conducts and says the rhythm exercise. A strong stress should be made by both groups on their first beat and a lesser stress should be made upon the third beat. For Example:

Group One 1   2   3   4

Group Two TAH tee tee *tah* tah

RHYTHM EXERCISES (Students' Manual page 65)

Conduct and say the following:

a) 4 ♩ ♩ ⊓ ♩ | ⊓ ⊓ ♩ ♪ | ⊓ ♩ ♩ | ⊓ ⊓ ♩ ♪ ‖

b) 4 ♩ ⊓ ⊓ ♪ | ♩ ♩ ⊓ ♩ | ⊓ ⊓ ♩ ♩ | ♩ ⊓ ♩ ♪ ‖

c) 4 ♩ ♩ ♩ | ⊓ ⊓ ♩ | ⊓ ♩ ♩ | ⊓ ⊓ ♩ ‖

d) 4 ⊓ ⊓ ♩ ♩ | ⊓ ⊓ ♩ | ⊓ ♩ ♪⊓ | ⊓ ⊓ ♩ ‖

e) 4 ♩ ♩ ♩ | ⊓ ♩ ♪ ♩ | ♩ ⊓ ⊓ | ⊓ ♩ ♩ ‖

f) 4 ♩. ♩ | ♩ ⊓ ♩ ♪ | ♩. ⊓ | ⊓ ⊓ ♩ ♪ ‖

g) 4 ♩ ♪ ⊓ ♪ | ⊓ ♩ ♪⊓♪⊓ | ♩ ♩ ♪⊓⊓ | ♩ ⊓ ♪⊓ ‖

h) 4 ♩ ⊓ ♩ ♩ | ♩. ♪ | ⊓ ♩ ♪⊓ | ♩. ♪ ‖

Rhythm Dictation

SUGGESTED PROCEDURES

1. The following (and similar) rhythm phrases can be dictated in two measure units to make the memorization simpler. The rhythms should be played so that the strong stress on the first beat and the lesser stress upon the third beat can be clearly presented.

a) 4 ♩ ♩ ♩ | ♩ ⊓ ♩ | ⊓ ♩ ⊓ ♩ | ♩ ♩ ♩ ‖

b) 4 ♩ ♩ | ♩ ♩ ♩ | ♩ ♩ ⊓ ⊓ | ⊓ ⊓ ♩ ‖

c) 4 ♩ ⊓ ♩ ♩ | ⊓ ♩ ♪ ♩ | ⊓ ♪⊓ ♩ | ⊓ ♩ ⊓ ♪ ‖

2. Play or tap rhythms from Unit Eleven and preceding units so that the class can determine the various meters (Duple, Triple, and Quadruple) of the examples.

Summary of Time Values of Notes and Equivalent Rests

This chart appears in the Students' Manual page 66.

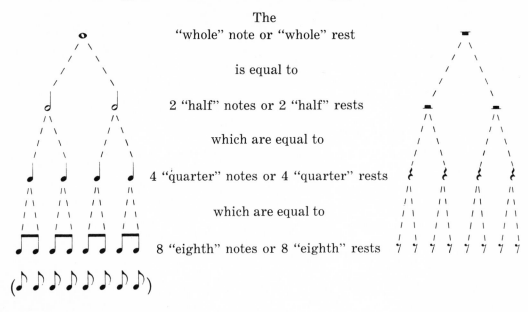

The
"whole" note or "whole" rest

is equal to

2 "half" notes or 2 "half" rests

which are equal to

4 "quarter" notes or 4 "quarter" rests

which are equal to

8 "eighth" notes or 8 "eighth" rests

SINGING EXERCISES (Students' Manual page 66)

Use several ways to interest the students in these exercises. Have them say the rhythm while conducting the time; sing each melody with hand signals or while they conduct. Try other devices we have suggested for singing exercises and whenever possible invent some game the children will enjoy playing as they learn rhythm and melody.

d) MMRM DL,M LLSL MRD'
LLSL MSMR MMRM L,L,L,

e) MMSL L D'D'LSL
SSMR R MMSSL

f) LLSL SMRM LSMR RMDD
LSMR MRDM MMRM L,L,L,L,

Hungarian Folk Song

Two-Part Melodies

a) Group One

SSLL S SSLL S D'D'D'D'S L SSSS D'

Group Two

SS MRD DRMM SD SSMR D

b) Group One

S MS D S L SM R

Group Two

S MRDRM L SM

DRMM S D'L SS S D
SS DRM MR D

101

SIGHT SINGING MELODIES (Students' Manual page 67)

Practice the Sight Singing Melodies in the following manner:
- a) Say the syllable names in rhythm.
- b) Sing the melodies with hand signals.
- c) Conduct the melodies while singing without hand signals.
- d) Determine the range of the melody and the type of scale (**La** or **Do**).

THE BIG CORRAL

ASSIGNMENT (Students' Manual page 69)

1. Compose melodies for any two Rhythm Exercises.
2. Compose two original melodies, four measures long. The first melody will begin on **So** and end on **Do**; the second melody will begin on **Do** and end on **La**.
3. Write Singing Exercises a) and c) on the staff. **Do** is in the first space.
4. Practice tapping the Rhythm Exercises with two hands. The left hand evenly taps four quarter (tah) notes per measure while the right hand taps the rhythm exercise as written.
5. Practice singing and conducting the rote song, "Colorado Trail."

Unit Twelve

Song Presentation

ROTE SONG

Teach this new rote song. Review again the section on "Teaching Songs" in the Introduction.

PRETTY SARO

Kentucky Folk Song

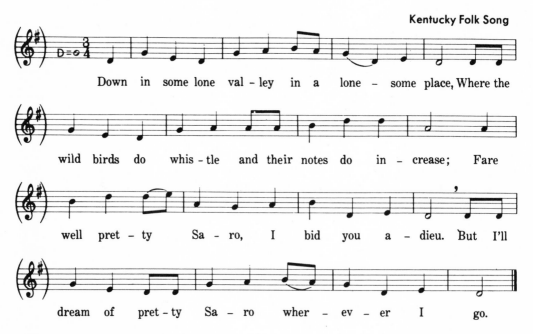

Down in some lone val - ley in a lone - some place, Where the

wild birds do whis - tle and their notes do in - crease; Fare

well pret - ty Sa - ro, I bid you a - dieu. But I'll

dream of pret - ty Sa - ro wher - ev - er I go.

SUGGESTED PROCEDURES

1. After the song has been learned, aid the class in discovering the syllable names of the notes.
2. Ask the class how many different syllables are contained in the song. They will find the five notes of the Pentatonic scale. Which of the five notes is the most important in the song? The syllable "So" is not only the first and last note, but is also used more often than any other (19 times).

104

3. Have the class sing a pentatonic scale beginning with low **So** and continuing

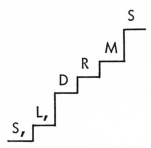

up to the next **So:**

4. Explain that although the **La** and **Do** are the two most common places upon which to build the pentatonic scale, *any syllable* can be the starting note.

5. Have the class sing the following pentatonic scales with hand signals:

a) "La" Pentatonic Scale: L, D R M S L' L S M R D L,

b) "Do" Pentatonic Scale: D R M S L D'' D' L S M R D

c) "Re" Pentatonic Scale: R M S L D' R'' R' D' L S M R

d) "Mi" Pentatonic Scale: M S L D' R' M'' M' R' D' L S M

e) "So" Pentatonic Scale: S, L, D R M S' S M R D L, S,

SINGING EXERCISES (Students' Manual page 72)

a) 4

L S M M S | L L S L M | R D L, L, D | R R D R L, ||

b) 4

D D R M S | L L L S | D' D' L S L | S S M S D' ||

c) 4

R' R' D' L S | L L S L | S S M R M | S S M R ||

d) 3

M M S L | D' D' R' R' | M' R' D' L | S S L '|

D' L D' L | S ' M M | L L S L | M. ||

e) 3 | | | | ♩ | ♩ | ♩' | | | | ♩ | | | | ♩ ⸸
   S M R D R D L, S, D R R R M R D D L, S,

f) 4 | ☐ | | | ☐ ♩' | ☐ | | | | | ♩'
   L S S L M R M S M L S S M R M D L,

   | ☐ | | | ☐ | ⸸ | ☐ | | | | ♩
   R R R D R M S S M R R R D R L, L, L,

Rhythm: The "Upbeat"

SUGGESTED PROCEDURES

1. Have the class sing the first four notes of "America the Beautiful" (Unit One). The class should determine which is the most important (stressed) sound — the word "O" or the word "beautiful."

2. Explain that when a piece begins upon an unstressed note, it is beginning upon a beat other than the first count of a measure. For example, "America the Beautiful" starts upon the fourth beat in Quadruple Time:

Beats 4 1	2	3	4	1	2	3	4	1	2	3	4	etc.
▬		⸸	O	beau –	ti-ful	for		spa –	cious	skies,	For	

It should be further explained that the piece is said to begin with an *upbeat* because of the position of the arm when conducting a beat other than the first, or *downward* arm motion.

3. Have the class sing "Auld Lang Syne" (Students' Manual page 73).

   a) The first measure must be clarified by explaining the symbol for the *half rest* (▬).

Count	1	2	3	4	1	2	3	4	1	2	3	4	1	2	3	4	1	2	3	4	1	2	3	4
Rhythm	▬		⸸	|	|	|	|	|	|	|	|	|	|	|	|	|	♩.			|	|	|	|	|
Syllables				S,	D	D	D	M	R	D	R	M	D	D	M	S	L			L	S	M	M	D

Count	1	2	3	4	1	2	3	4	1	2	3	4	1	2	3	4	1	2	3	4	1	2	3	4
Rhythm	|	|	|	|	|	|	|	|	♩		⸸	|	|	|	|	|	|	|	|	|	|	|	|	|
Syllables	R	D	R	M	D	L,	L,	S,	D			L	S	M	M	D	R	D	R	L	S	M	M	S

Count	1	2	3	4	1	2	3	4	1	2	3	4	1	2	3	4	1	2	3	4		
Rhythm	♩		⸸	|	|	|	|	|	|	|	|	|	|	|	|	|	♩.			⸸		
Syllables	L			L	S	M	M	D	R	D	R	M	D	L,	L,	S,	D					

b) After the song has been practiced, the first measure should be rewritten without the rests. The last measure will, therefore, balance the "incomplete" first measure by subtracting the last beat. The song has been *rewritten* this way as Sight Singing Melody No. 4.

a)

b)

c)

d)

e) Group One

Group Two

f) Group One

Group Two

Dictation

SUGGESTED PROCEDURES

1. Play short melodies such as the suggested ones below. The teacher must play or sing the sound of **Do**. The students should hum back the melody before writing the syllables. The rhythm is then to be memorized and written above the syllables.

S L S M D   D R D L, S,   D M R D L,   L L S M M L,

(Space is provided in students' book for writing these dictation patterns.)

1. Sing the following canon in two parts. It is composed of the three notes of the major **(Do)** triad:

4 | ① | | ⊓ | | ② | | | ⅆ || | | ⊓ | | | | ⅆ |
S M S M D |M S S |D' S M M S |M D D |

| | ⊓ | | | | ⅆ || | | ⊓ | | | | ⅆ ‖
D' S M M S |D'D' S |M S M M D |M S D

2. Now sing the canon again, but this time it is composed of the three notes of the minor **(La)** triad:

4 | ① | | ⊓ | | ② | | | ⅆ || | | ⊓ | | | | ⅆ |
M D M D L, |D M M |L M D D M |D L, L, |

| | ⊓ | | | | ⅆ || | | ⊓ | | | | ⅆ ‖
L M D D M |L L M |D M D D L, |D M L,

SIGHT SINGING MELODIES (Students' Manual page 75)

First practice the following melodies with hand signals; then conduct and sing without hand signals.

1. D=o 4   *p*

2. D=o 2   *mf*

Hungarian Folk Song

3. D=o 2   *p*

108

4.

ASSIGNMENT (Students' Manual page 76)

1. Sing the **La, Do, Re, Mi,** and **So** Pentatonic Scales, up and down, in the following rhythms. The "La" Pentatonic Scale has been written below as a guide:

a) 2   L, DR | M S | L ' | L | S M R D | L,

b) 2   L,D R | M S L | L   S | M R   D | L,

2. Memorize Sight Singing Melody No. 2. Sing it by heart while pointing to the correct notes on the music staff below:

Notes For Sight Singing Melody No. 2

3. Write Singing Exercise c) on the staff. **Do** is the first space.
4. Practice Rhythm Exercises e) and f) with the right tapping the upper rhythm part and the left hand tapping the lower part.

With the completion of Unit Twelve we reach the first goal of SIGHT AND SOUND. The students have worked with various elements of music but in particular the Pentatonic Scale, the basis for the major-minor system. In future units we will progress to the aural and written uses of the major and minor keys as well as the utilization of accidentals and modulation. More part singing will be practical because the seeds of good intonation have been sown ; rhythms and meters of greater complexity have also been prepared for. In the units which will follow in the second book we will continue to develop the concepts of aural musicianship.